Design for Assembly

Design for Assembly

M. Myrup Andreasen   IPU
S. Kähler   IPU/DT
T. Lund   DT

IPU : The Institute for Product
      Development
      The Technical University of
      Denmark

DT : Danish Technology Ltd.

IFS (Publications) Ltd., U.K.

Springer-Verlag,
Berlin, Heidelberg, New York, Tokyo

1983

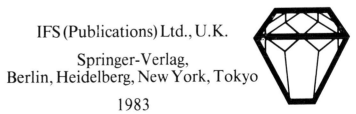

British Library Cataloguing Publication Data

Andreasen, M. Myrup
  Design for assembly.
1. Production engineering
I. Title II. Kahler, S. III. Lund, T.
621.7   TS176
ISBN 0-903608-35-9 IFS (Publications) Ltd.
ISBN 3-540-12544-2 Springer-Verlag. Berlin. Heidelberg. New York. Tokyo.
ISBN 0-387-12544-2 New York. Heidelberg. Berlin. Tokyo.

Typesetting by Fotographics (Bedford) Limited.
Printed by Cotswold Press, Oxford, England.

Author's Preface

The designer plays a key role in the development and rationalisation of the field of assembly. If the designs are not good from the assembly standpoint, rationalisation of the chain of assembly will only be of limited success.

This book is perceived as an introduction to the assembly process and design for ease of assembly with emphasis on mechanised and automatic assembly.

The book shows the principles and directives for the structuring and designing of products with a view to ease of assembly. In addition, a series of general factors and principles exerting a degree of influence on the success of an assembly rationalisation project are dealt with.

This book can be used in "teach-yourself" courses, in so far as the experienced designer will be able to apply the many examples to his or her own situation. The book can additionally be used as course material, and we hope, as a text for those studying engineering in technical colleges and universities.

If you have any questions or comments to the text or the many examples, or would like to discuss design of products or design of assembly machines please do not hesitate to contact us by phone or mail at: Danish Technology Ltd., Birkehavevej 3, DK 3760 Birkeroed, Denmark. Phone +45 2 815300.

Lyngby, Denmark
November 1982

Mogens Myrup Andreasen/Steen Kähler/Thomas Lund

Contents

Rationalising assembly

– does the need exist?

SUMMARY

In recent decades the development of production technique has taken place considerably quicker in the realm of component manufacture than in that of assembly.

As a rule assembly is carried out manually and typically accounts for between 40 and 60% of the total production time.

Increasing demands for greater job content, improved working environment and higher wages mean that we must develop new areas of rationalisation in orders to increase productivity; only by means of this will be possible to maintain or increase competitiveness and consequently employment.

Increased productivity can be achieved by applying new methods of organisation and production principles in addition to increased mechanisation and automation.

The most effective opportunities for rationalisation however, can be attained by regarding assembly as part of the total production system and not as an individual entity. Design offers such opportunities.

1.1 Does the need exist?

Production technique development has taken place considerably quicker in the realm of component manufacture than in that of assembly. The assembly sector's wage share has therefore steadily increased.

Progress in component manufacture

Increased productivity in this sector has been achieved with the aid of considerable technical progress – examples of such being:

★ Application of highly productive processes such as extrusion, powder metallurgy, pressure die casting and injection moulding.

★ Utilisation of new cutting materials such as hard metal and ceramics in the cutting field.

★ Use of numerically controlled machine tools.

★ Application of revolutionary concepts such as a machining centre and an integrated yet flexible production plant.

★ Utilisation of new processes such as spark machining and electro-chemical processing.

Progress in assembly

The technical development of assembly equipment is relatively slow and by no means comparable to that of processing.

Most assembly work is executed manually with the aid of few tools. Typically 40 to 60% of the total production period is occupied by assembly.

Increased productivity in the assembly sector has been achieved by rationalisation in the form of:

★ Increased use of assembly lines.

★ Increased division of work.

★ Widespread use of methods related to time and motion studies (e.g. MTM).

Increased productivity can be partly achieved through a more effective exploitation of the man-machine combination, although developments over the past few years indicate that this has its limitations.

Increasing demands for greater job content, improved working conditions and higher wages mean that we must develop new areas of rationalisation in order to increase productivity; only by means of this will it be possible to maintain or increase competitiveness and consequently employment.

The alternative is that potential products are shelved or at best developed domestically but manufactured abroad.

Thus one can entertain no doubts as to the validity of the title question: "does the need exist?" – most definitely yes!

1.2 In which areas?

Several areas present themselves – some actually part of the assembly process, others in the remaining sectors of the firm.

New organisation and production principles combined with increased mechanisation and automation can bring about a rationalisation of the assembly process. Consequently a better working environment, greater job content and satisfaction can be attained.

The most effective opportunities for rationalisation however, can be attained by regarding assembly as part of the entire production system and not as an individual entity. The area of design and its relationships with component production offer such opportunities.

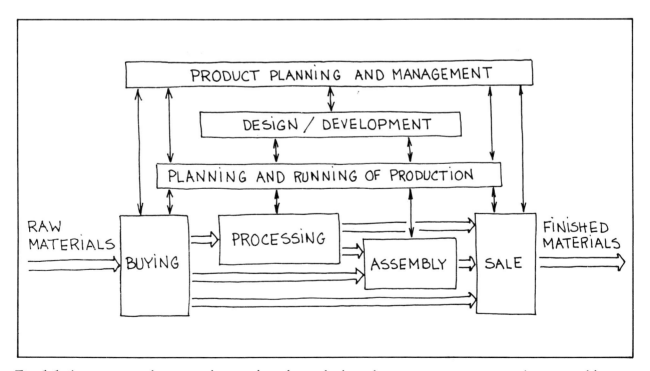

Fig. 1.1. An integrated approach must be adopted when the intention is to rationalise assembly.

Relationship to component manufacture

Assembly and component manufacture are closely related throughout a material stream – namely those components which make up assembly.

Problems such as:

★   Interruption of component supply

★   Burrs

★   Exceeding limits of tolerance

★   Dirt and foreign bodies

★   Deficient processing

★   Erroneous processing

will cause many assembly problems and all stem from the processing sector.

Other problems traceable to the processing sector are those caused by the particular production technique applied. If a product, for example, is built from punched and bent sheet metal parts which are welded together, it will have to be assembled. Such an assembly can be eliminated by means of pressure die casting.

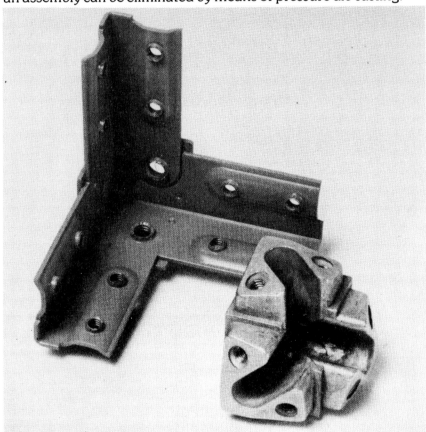

Fig 1.2. Assembly can be eliminated in certain cases by adoption of a different technique. A simple example is illustrated above. This corner element for casing components from Løgstrup was previously produced by welding such sheet metal parts. Today it is a pressure die casting.

Relationship to design:

The product's design determines its structure, method of assembly, number of components, component design, choice of material, tolerances and surface finishes, etc. Assembly is thus fundamentally established during the design phase. Unfortunately one encounters all too often the designer who takes no great notice of assembly – he is preoccupied with achieving the desired product function.

This is in spite of the fact that it is in the design phase that the problems –and thereby expenses – arise. Fig. 1.3 illustrates the cost distribution in a typical production system.

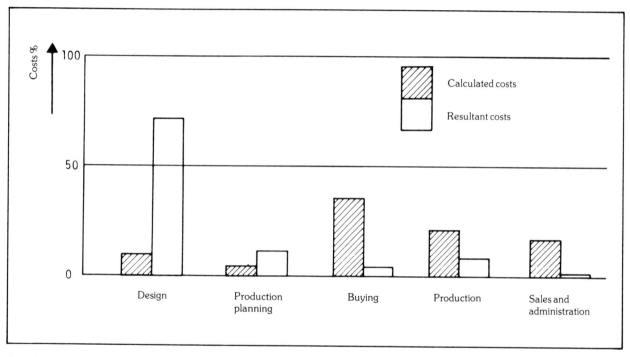

Fig. 1.3. The distribution among departments of the calculated and the resultant costs.

The lack of consideration given to assembly in the fields of component design and product structure can be put down to:

★   Lack of time or deficient time planning

★   Lack of realisation as to importance of assembly

★   Lack of knowledge of design oriented assembly.

★   The habit of saying "they usually work it out in production".

★   Organisational problems which restrict a fruitful co-operation between employees from various functional areas.

13

Thus considerable opportunities for rationalisation exist – to such an extent that function, production and assembly can be regarded as a whole. Furthermore it is important to recognise that product design is not only a question of ensuring that the product achieves the desired function but also a question of:

★   What shall the components be produced of? (input)

★   How shall they be produced?

★   How shall they be assembled?

This is illustrated in Fig. 1.4.

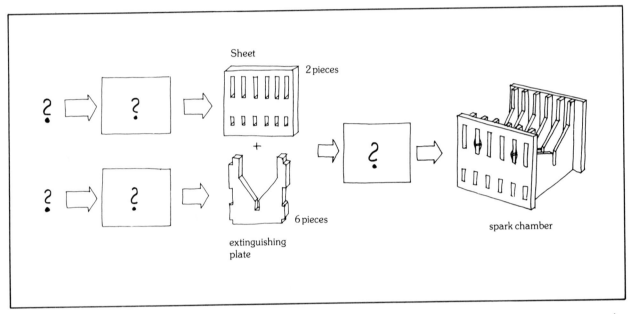

Fig. 1.4. Product design goes some way in replying to the question concerning starting materials, mode of component production and method of assembly. The product shown is a spark chamber from an LK-NES automatic relay type M34.

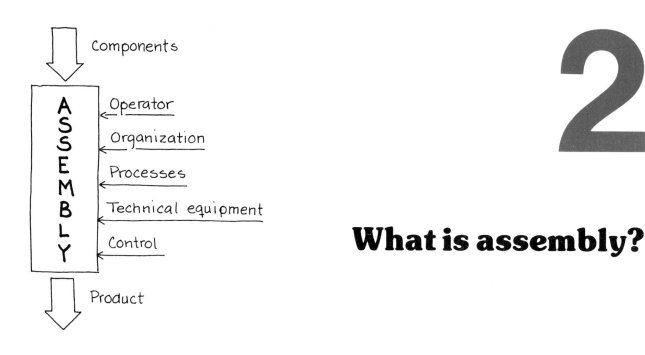

2

What is assembly?

SUMMARY

The concept of the word "assembly" differs from firm to firm and it is therefore impossible to answer the question "what is assembly?" definitively. It can be safely assumed however that assembly is a major part of the total production process.

Assembly functions can be divided into constituent functions – handling, composing and checking. These are described in greater detail in Chapter 3.

The following factors justify assembly from the functional and design points of view: required are degrees of freedom (movement), differentiation of material, production considerations of material, production considerations, establishment considerations, differentiation of functions, relation of functions and finally design considerations.

2.1 What is assembly?

Industrial production can be divided into the manufacture of raw and finished materials in addition to assembly. See Fig. 2.1.

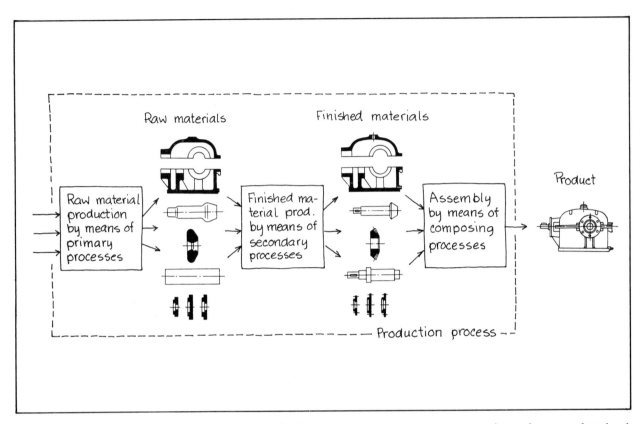

Fig. 2.1. Industrial production can be divided into three stages: raw material production, finished material production and assembly.

The final principal part of the production process is the joining of the materials. The product gradually takes shape in the form of machined parts, components and sub-assemblies in a complex process termed "assembly".

By machined parts is meant individual unjoined parts. Those objects utilised in the assembly process are characterised by the words component and sub-assembly, see Fig. 2.2. A component can be purely a machined part or a compound as a result of assembly.

Assembly's main function is to join components, formless material and sub-assemblies into a complex product. Achieving this by use of screws is regarded as a process including machined parts, the screws not being regarded as a particular joining element. Gathering, filling and covering of surfaces including packaging can be regarded as composing processes, but not normally as an assembly operation.

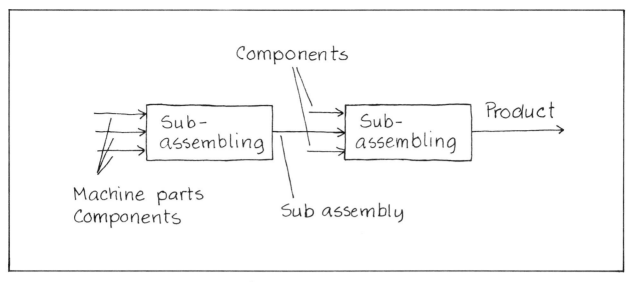

Fig. 2.2. Some important designations. See also Chapter 3.

Joining can be achieved by:

means of shape, e.g. supporting, lead-in, wrapping, in-laying, filling, etc.

means of force, e.g. with the aid of friction or field force (inertia, magnetism, etc.).

means of material, e.g. bonding, welding, etc.

A survey of joining methods categorised from other standpoints is shown below.

★ Composing by <u>joining</u>, e.g. enclose, in-laying, sliding in, hanging, etc.

★ Composing by <u>filling</u> (of cavity), e.g. with gas, liquid, formless material.

★ Composing by <u>interference</u>, e.g. wedging, screwing, squeezing, shrinking, forcing, riveting, nailing, etc.

★ Composing by <u>phase changes</u>, e.g. casting, forging, etc.

★ Composing by <u>change of form</u>, e.g. riveting, folding, swaging, beading, clenching, rolling, etc.

★ Composing by <u>means of material</u>, e.g. welding, soldering, glueing, plating, metal spraying, etc.

★ Composing <u>by other means</u>, e.g. sewing, tying, wrapping, splicing, weaving, braiding, etc.

Fig. 2.3. shows the various classes of assembly objects – correspondingly the assembly tasks can vary greatly as in the case of a fuel valve, a fuel pump, a diesel motor and a diesel electric locomotive. (Please note that all of these products appear as elements later).

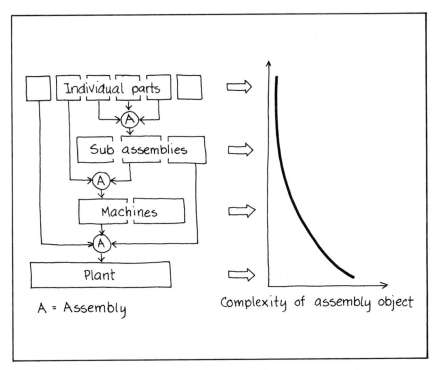

Fig. 2.3. Assembly objects can be divided into various classes.

The actual assembly function can be divided into constituent functions:

> Handling
> Composing
> Checking

The function of handling is to put two or more objects into a particular mutual position.

The function of composing is to ensure this mutual relationship against outside effects.

The checking function is to ascertain whether this has been carried out as specified.

Chapter 3 describes these in greater detail.

Unfortunately the concept "assembly" is as yet rather nebulous. It is perceived differently from firm to firm and branch to branch. It often acts as an umbrella for functions such as: construction, joining, erection, mounting or fitting synonymously with assembly.

The following chapters dealing with assembly pay particular attention to the fields of mechanical engineering and electronic industries. Some typical examples of assembly tasks in these fields are:

Construction of mechanical tools, agricultural machinery, special machines and bodies.

Construction of valves and compressors.

Construction of electrical building elements such as relays, contacts, switches and thermostats.

Construction of electrical apparatus, motors, etc.

However one must bear in mind that assembly also takes place in various areas of commerce such as the textile industry (sewing), brewing (tapping, labelling and capping), and the building industry.

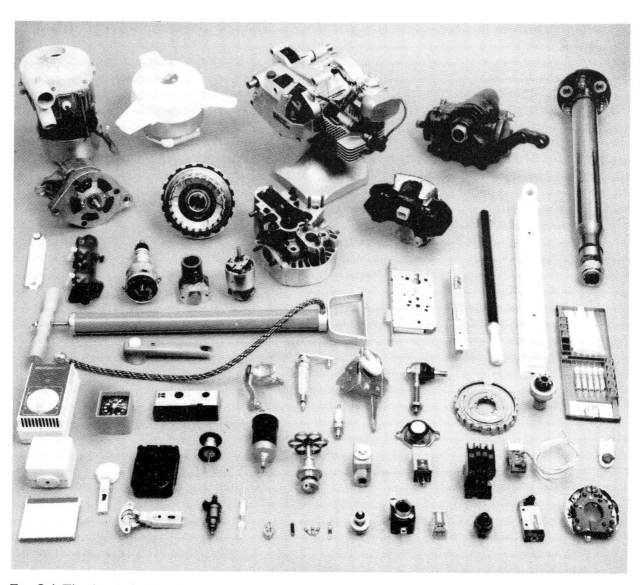

Fig. 2.4. This book deals with the assembly of the above products. (BOSCH).

2.2 Why assemble?

As mentioned in Chapter 1 assembly is often both expensive and complicated – so why not design products in order to avoid assembly?

This is often possible with "simple" products but in the case of more advanced devices one must accept the necessity of assembly.

Why assemble?

A machine or a product's task is to carry out or provide particular functions. Fig. 2.5 illustrates a product whose function is to open or shut off a stream of liquid.

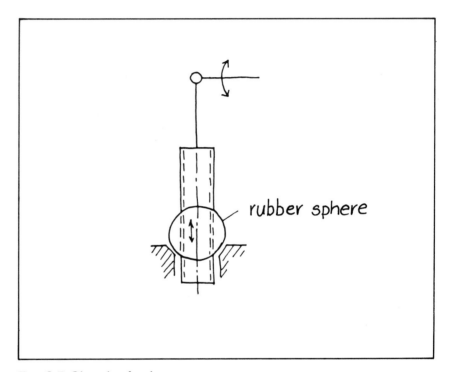

Fig. 2.5. Sketch of valve.

The conical surface and rubber sphere combine to allow closing. The cylindrical surface together with the protruding pipe control the opening. The design is determined during the design phase and correspondingly the mode of production and to a significant extent assembly also. The results of design can be seen in Fig. 2.6.

The answer to the question "Why assemble?" can be gleaned from a comparison of the two illustrations. The points of interest are numbered on Figure 2.6 and discussed below.

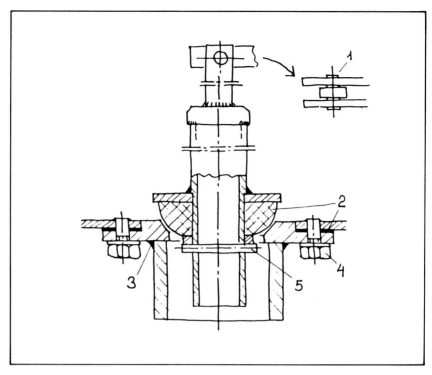

Fig. 2.6. Detailed sketch of valve.

1. DEGREES OF FREEDOM (MOVEMENT): Various elements must enjoy a degree of mobility in order to achieve the function (e.g. the pin at the top).

2. MATERIAL DIFFERENTIATION: The function's realisation depends on particular material characteristics (e.g. assembly of rubber and gasket).

3. PRODUCTION CONSIDERATIONS: Some parts will be easier to produce by division into sub-parts (e.g. the pipe and stationary sealing surface's division into two, to be assembled by welding).

4. ESTABLISHMENT CONSIDERATIONS (REPLACE-ABILITY): The product may be used in a fixed installation and have to be assembled in a separate process (e.g. assembly of closing system by bolting).

5. DIFFERENTIATION OF FUNCTIONS: A function can be carried out by a single agent or a combination of such in the form of more elements (e.g. the rubber element's fixing in a ring by means of a pin, the ring distributing the force).

6. PARTICULAR FUNCTIONAL CONDITIONS: In the sense of increased requirements of accessibility, demounting, cleansing, inspection, etc. These can necessitate a division into elements.

7. DESIGN CONSIDERATIONS: Aesthetic requirements can cause a division of the form which will consequently require assembly.

It is vital that the designer bears these factors in mind during the basic design phase – only then will it be possible to group function, production and assembly under a simple umbrella.

Simple examples of such alternative product designs during which such considerations have been taken into account are shown below and on the following page.

Alternative possibilities

An optimal design – also from the assembly point of view can only be achieved by considering the alternative possibilities, which in turn can provide degrees of design freedom.

Alternatives can be created by considering various form divisions. See Fig. 2.7 and Chapters 5-8.

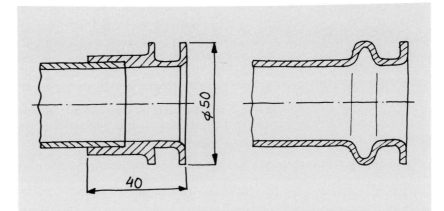

Illustrated two pipe stubs (A) to the left has been assembled. (B) to the right has not.

(A) is produced by machining – the drawbacks being: considerable production time, large use of material (waste) and assembly time.

(B) is produced by deformation shaping and includes none of the above-mentioned disadvantages.

On the other hand it is conceivable that (A) is preferable to (B) if one lacks the necessary technique required for (B)'s production – point 3 on page 21.

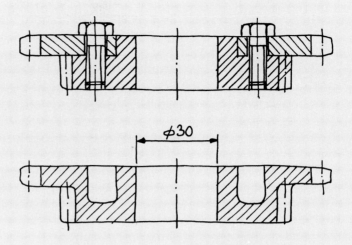

Illustrated are two different types of combined sprocket and gear wheel. A includes assembly, B does not.

A is made of steel and produced by machining. The individual teeth are cut. It is necessary to divide A into two elements –in a nutshell assembly due to production technique reasons.

B is produced from sinter metal – the teeth being sintered in accordance with the required tolerance and surface quality; the advantages being no waste material, short processing time and no assembly.

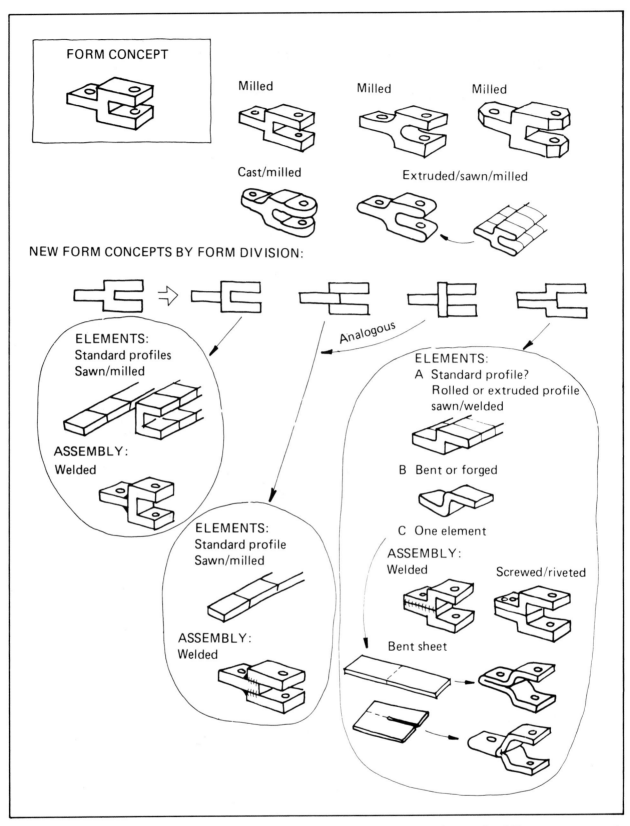

Fig. 2.7. The illustrated fork element can be produced by means of greatly differing input with accompanying production processes including assembly. (4).

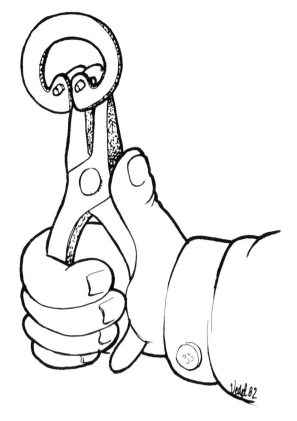

3

Assembly operations and equipment

SUMMARY

In the assembly process machine parts, components, building blocks, base components and in some cases auxiliary material combine to form the product.

This takes place gradually through a series of operations termed sub-assemblies. Ultimately the product appears as a result of the final assembly.

The three main stages in the assembly process are: handling, composing and checking. These can be sub-divided into storage, transport and positioning which can in turn be sub-divided if required.

Product assembly can thus be modelled with the aid of symbols, sketches or verbal blocks.

Typical assembly equipment is shown at the end of the chapter.

Automatic assembly

Fig. 3.1. Automatic assembly of electric switches, deisgned and built by LK-NES process switches techniques, Denmark.

3.1 The assembly process

Under this heading we will examine the complexity of the process and its integration into other facets of the production process. A product is normally made up of many machine parts which are put together in an exact sequence, during which they are checked, painted, adjusted and shaped before the final assembly operation is achieved.

It is necessary to differentiate between the various objects which are realised in the assembly process:

Machine part:	Is composed of a single material and is an individual part of the machine or product.
Component:	Ranges from a machine part to a combination of parts which are included in the product.
Building block:	A composite part of the product which because of assembly requirements represents a sub-assembly.
Base component:	A (larger) component onto which others are assembled.
Formless material:	e.g. viscose components such as glue, paint, liquids.

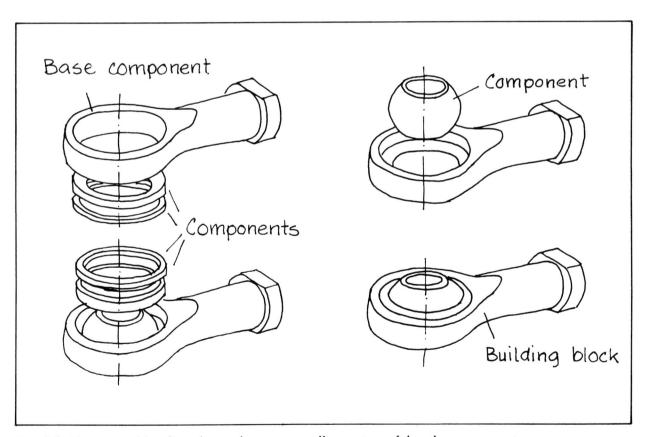

Fig. 3.2. The assembly of a spherical joint as an illustration of the above concepts.

Product assembly

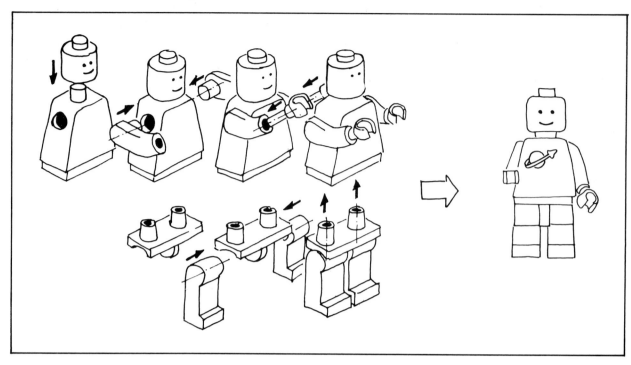

Fig. 3.3. Step by step assembly of spaceman from Lego Ltd.

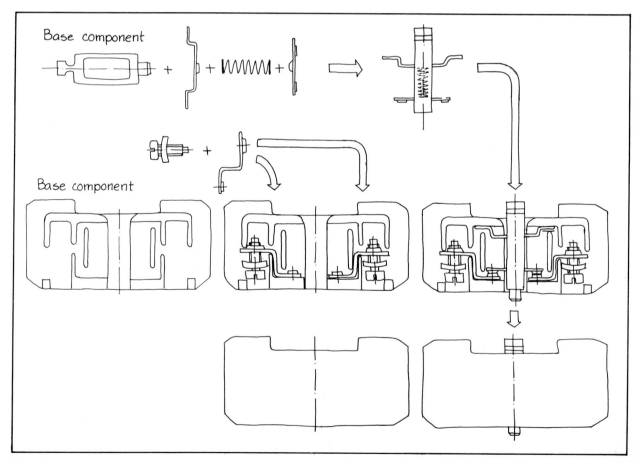

Fig. 3.4. Step by step assembly of switch from Danfos Ltd. The components act as guides for the upper part which is ultrasonically welded to the base component.

Fig. 3.2 illustrates how a larger machine part can represent a base component. The finished result can be perceived as a building block as it is an assembled element of the consequent assembly.

Figs. 3.3 and 3.4 illustrate product assembly partly without base components and partly a typical "inlaying" assembly with base components, where the components guide the upper part.

Division of the assembly process (complexity)

The assembly of a complex product is the result of several steps. It can be of some importance to differentiate between these and the final assembly for instance where this final assembly leads to product variations. The two concepts can be defined as:

Sub-assembly:	An individual assembly operation where one component is assembled with another component, a base component or a building block.
Final assembly:	Describes the construction of a building block or the finished product.

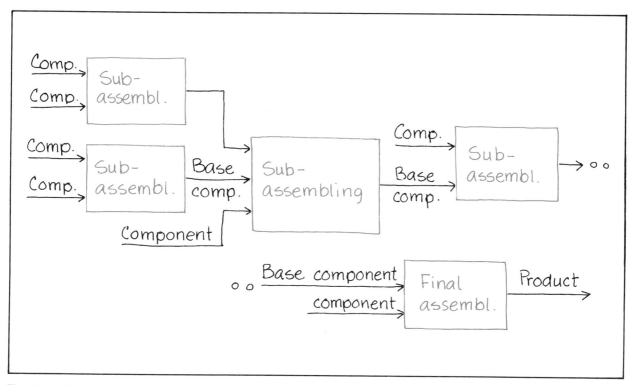

Fig. 3.5. The concepts of sub and final assembly illustrated in a process model. As in Fig. 3.4 a single component can be perceived as a base component.

The assembly system can be integrated with processing, transport, packaging and testing equipment.

Integrated processes

Various processes, e.g. component production, testing, adjusting, surface treating and sorting can take place between the assembly stages. This can be a necessity either because later assembly will render such a procedure impossible or by reason of design advantages, e.g. a surface treatment could be easily integrated with the assembly equipment; blanking of a component can be achieved so that the component can be directly transferred to the site of assembly so that handling is avoided.

The assembly process is thus directed by the product's components, the type of construction and the degree of integration required with the other processes. Each assembly operation requires the execution of a series of auxiliary processes.

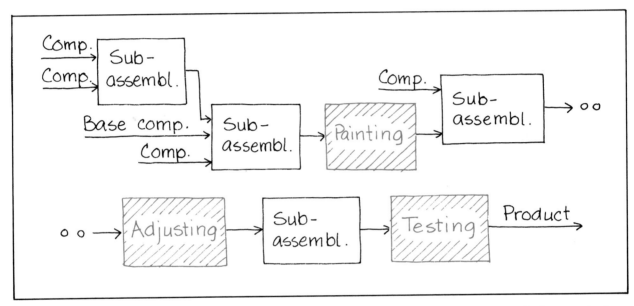

Fig. 3.6. General process model of assembly with integrated processes, including painting, adjusting and testing. These operations can occasionally be profitably integrated into the assembly system.

3.2 Assembly operations

Experience shows that every assembly includes a limited number of operations. These "standard" operations are illustrated in Fig. 3.7. The sub-processes of the entire assembly process will be one or more of the "handling", "composing" or "checking" processes. All three part processes however will be composed of a series of operations among which are storing, transporting and positioning which can in turn be sub-divided.

Special processes, such as adjusting, surface treating and packaging can be incorporated into the assembly process, depending upon the assembly system's degree of integration with pre- and succeeding processes.

Assembly operations

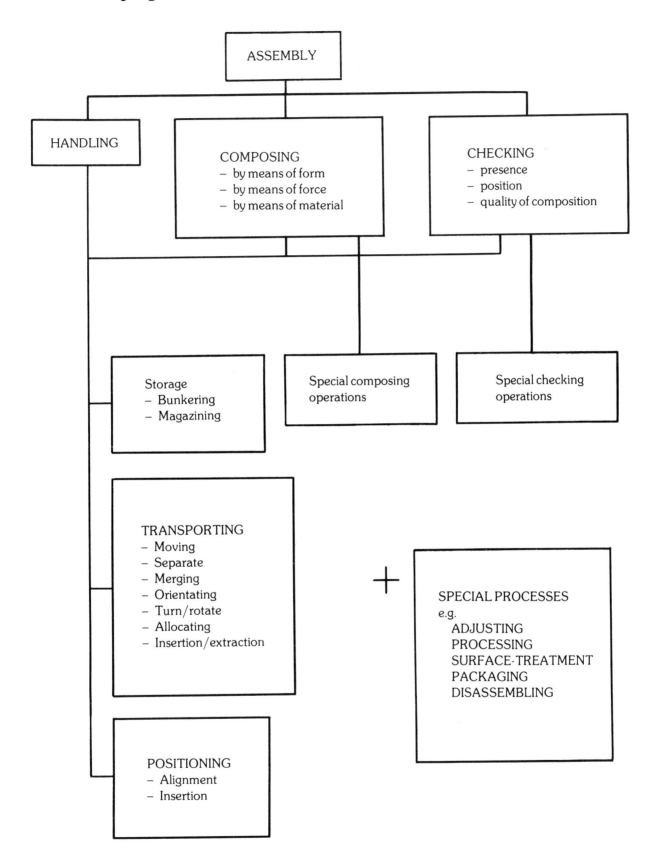

Fig. 3.7. An assembly process is a compound of handling, composing and checking, as well as special processes if required. These processes can be sub-divided into storage, transport and positioning as well as special operations connected to composing, checking, etc.

Handling

Storage

The time-oriented process by which components are stored before or after handling, composing and checking.

Hopper Storage

Time-oriented storage of components as yet unoriented.

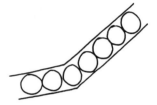

Magazining

Time-oriented storage of oriented components.

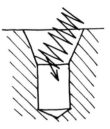

Positioning

The process with the aim of orientating one component in relation to another.

Alignment

Positioning of component in one or more axial directions in relation to the base component.

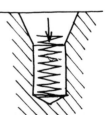

Insertion

Relocation of component in relation to base component resulting in the terminal position.

Transporting

Process with the aim of moving and orientating components according to the demands of the composition and checking processes.

Moving

Constant or indexing relocation within the assembly system.
If this operation is carried out by an operator or robot there will be three phases: recognition, gripping and moving.

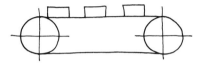

Separating

Division of a single stream of components into many streams.

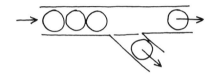

Merge

Merging of two or more streams of components.

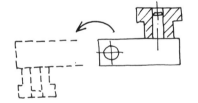

Orientation

Orientation of stream of components in relation to the system.

Turning/rotating

Orientation of components within stream in relation to system.

Allocating

Release of a given number of components from stream, to the system.

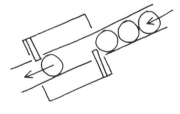

Insertion/Extraction

Positioning of component in the tool, removal of component.

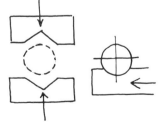

The determination of the assembly system (Chapter 4) is based on a model of the operations within the assembly process. We feel it is prudent to examine the applied concepts of handling, composing and testing in greater detail. (Examples of which appear on pages 32 and 33.)

Process modelling with verbal blocks

An assembly process can be modelled or described on the basis of the operations shown on pages 32 and 33. This can be achieved with the aid of block diagrams, symbols or sketches.

Assembly

Handling

Processes of selection and preparation of components for composing or checking and transportation to the following production, assembly or packaging systems. For sub-process see Fig. 3.7.

Composing

The aim of which is to create a (relatively) permanent connection between the components. The composition process can be achieved by means of shape, force or material.

Checking

Processes by which the component's presence and position is checked in addition to the finished product's quality. Sub-processes can include handling in addition to special checking operations (e.g. measuring, comparison and rejection). If additional handling or composing operations are required subsequent to checking one can speak of ADJUSTING.

We recommend modelling with 'verbal' blocks. We feel symbolic language is too abstract, consequently difficult to learn and lacks sufficient symbols to account for the many assembly operations.

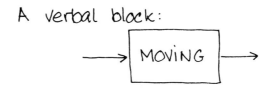

A verbal block:

It is important to model an assembly process because in this way an objective starting point for assembly considerations can be created. The following important principles apply to the modelling of an assembly process.

1. The components are successive throughout the process model, i.e. the arrows are components in particular states (unoriented, oriented...) the boxes represent operations which enable the transfer of components from one state to another.

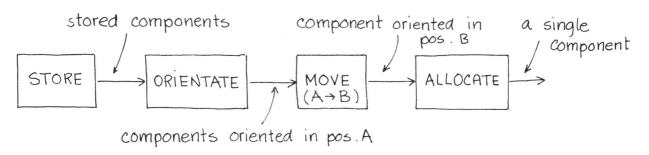

2. It is conceivable that several sub-processes can be realised simultaneously without necessitating succession. In this case the "process boxes" are parallel.

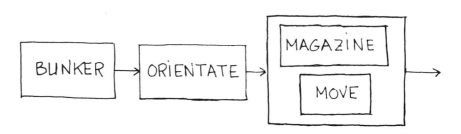

See examples on pages 36 and 37.

Other model types

It can be advisable to implement other more pictorial model forms during the design determination of the assembly. It would be superfluous to examine this point any further, or to describe the symbol language widely used in Germany for describing assembly processes. Those interested can however refer to (6).

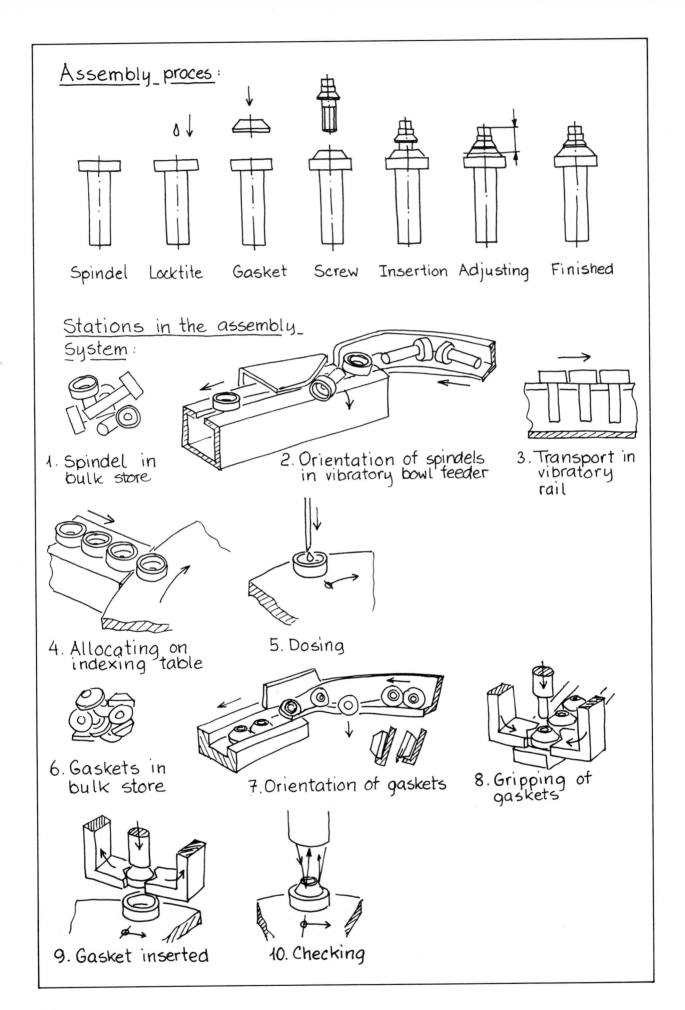

Assembly proces:

Spindel   Locktite   Gasket   Screw   Insertion   Adjusting   Finished

Stations in the assembly System:

1. Spindel in bulk store

2. Orientation of spindels in vibratory bowl feeder

3. Transport in vibratory rail

4. Allocating on indexing table

5. Dosing

6. Gaskets in bulk store

7. Orientation of gaskets

8. Gripping of gaskets

9. Gasket inserted

10. Checking

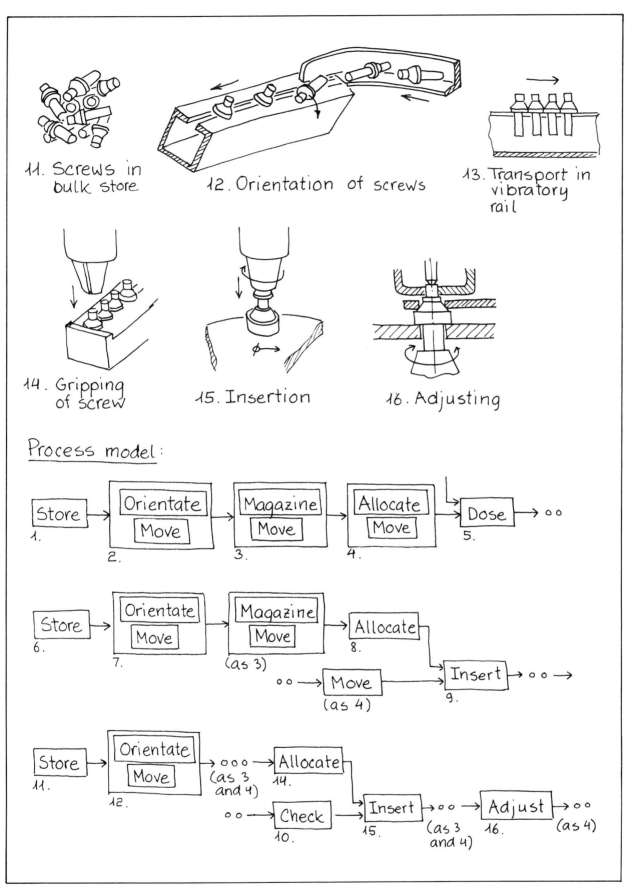

11. Screws in bulk store

12. Orientation of screws

13. Transport in vibratory rail

14. Gripping of screw

15. Insertion

16. Adjusting

Process model:

Store 1. → Orientate / Move 2. → Magazine / Move 3. → Allocate / Move 4. → Dose 5. → ∘∘

Store 6. → Orientate / Move 7. → Magazine / Move (as 3) → Allocate 8. → Insert 9. → ∘∘ →
∘∘ → Move (as 4) → Insert 9.

Store 11. → Orientate / Move 12. → ∘∘∘ (as 3 and 4) → Allocate 14. → Insert 15. → ∘∘ (as 3 and 4) → Adjust 16. → ∘∘ (as 4)
∘∘ → Check 10. → Insert 15.

Fig. 3.8. Spindle assembly as an illustration of assembly modelling. The assembly and adjustments of the components are shown first, followed by the most important stages in the assembly machine. The process model completes the sequence. (Some repetitions have been omitted.) The automatic assembly machine is shown in Chapter 4, page 60.

Assembly is also . . .

The concept of assembly is not restricted to the fields of mechanical technology. Certain processes in the grocery and clothing industries may be classed as assembly; these in turn may provide inspiration for the solution of problems related to tasks in mechanical assembly.

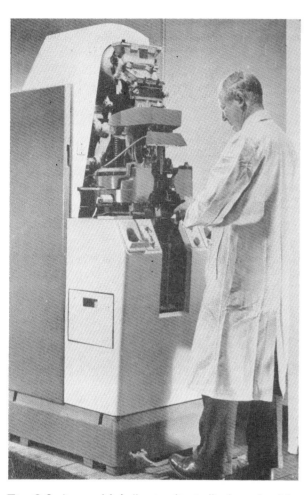

Fig. 3.9. Assembly's "outer limits" where highly developed technology may be of benefit: e.g. the shoe industry, musical instrument production and the packaging industry.

3.3 Assembly equipment

In section 3.2 we have seen how assembly consists of three sub-processes –handling, composing and checking.

A good deal of (standard) equipment is available today for each of these and their respective sub-divisions. Naturally one will encounter degrees of difference in the assembly equipment, corresponding to the type of assembly system implemented.

Assembly equipment ranges from the basic tools used in manual assembly to more complex fully automatic assembly lines. A selection of equipment is illustrated on the following pages. These are meant to show the application of the terminology from Fig. 3.7.

One can ascertain from the descriptions that the equipment can carry out many of the operations and procedures described in Fig. 3.7. A vibrating bowl feeder will, for example, be able to execute storage as well as transport (moving and orientating). It is important to bear this in mind during designing, only then can one achieve an optimal combination of product and assembly equipment, i.e. a product which from the assembly point of view is suited to the assembly equipment.

Storage of components on the table at manual assembly point.

★ STORING

Storage of components in trays at the manual assembly point.

★ STORING

Components stored in feeder which automatically transports them when circular bowl feeder is about to empty (IPU).

★ STORING
★ MOVING

Vibrating rail for transport of component, orientated between circular bowl feeder and indexing table (IPU).

    ★ MOVING
    ★ MAGAZINING

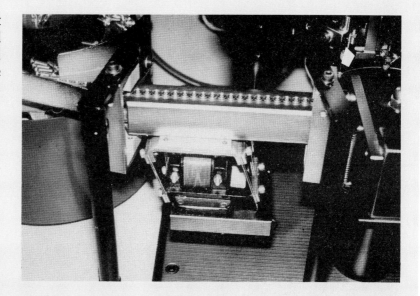

Chute for product transport from indexing table to storage box. A separation flap (for defective or erroneous products) has been built in (IPU).

    ★ MOVING
    ★ SEPARATING

Indexing table for component transport between process stations. It also functions as an escapement, taking components directly from a vibrating rail (IPU).

    ★ MOVING
    ★ ALLOCATING

41

Circular bowl feeders and other feeding equipment for springs (Vibradan/Menziken) mounted to an automatic assembly machine designed by LY-NES Process Technique, Denmark.

★ STORING
★ ORIENTATING
★ MAGAZINING
★ MOVING

Spring sorter for separation of tangled springs (Tekno-Detaljer AB).

★ STORING
★ SEPARATING

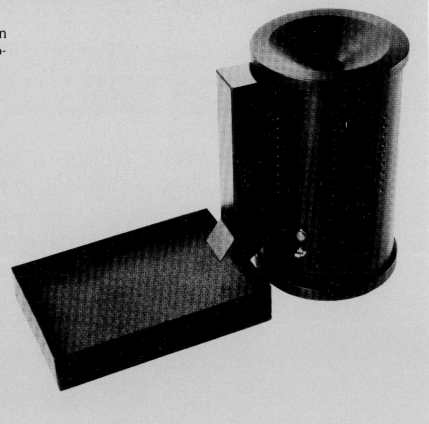

Pneumatic pick and place equipment, constructed from standard BOSCH equipment.

- ★ MOVING
- ★ ALLOCATING
- ★ INSERTION/ EXTRACTION

Autoscrewdriver from Aylesbury Automation whose main function is composing, but is capable of various operations, particularly when fitted, as shown here, with a vibrating bowl feeder.

- ★ STORING
- ★ ORIENTATING
- ★ MOVING
- ★ SEPARATING
- ★ ALLOCATING
- ★ COMPOSING

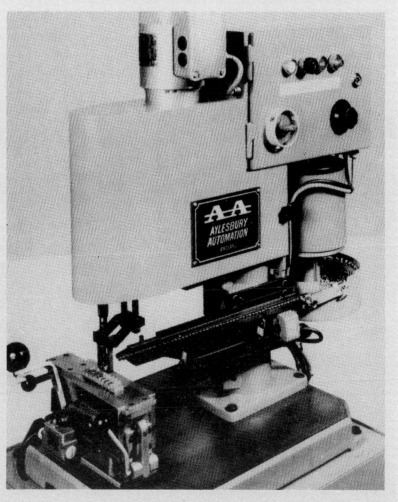

43

Thin plate composition by means of flap riveting. The Berama flap pistol illustrated stamps out and bends two flaps so that the plates are connected with their own material.

★ COMPOSING

Photocell checking of presence of paper in tobacco tins – if missing the tin will be rejected.

★ CHECKING
★ SEPARATING

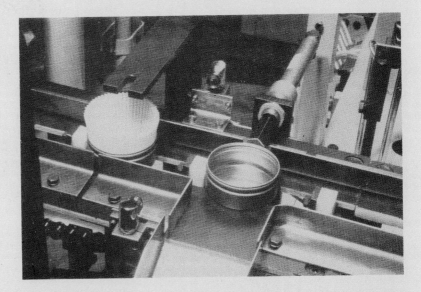

Tampoprint printing on packaging. This equipment is part of the group of special processes in Fig. 3.7.

★ SURFACE
  TREATING

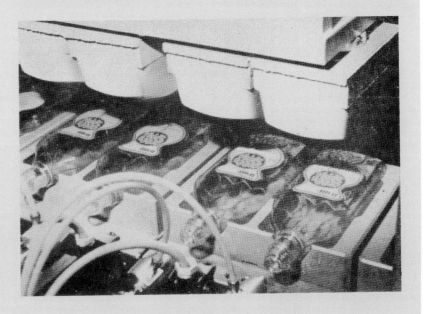

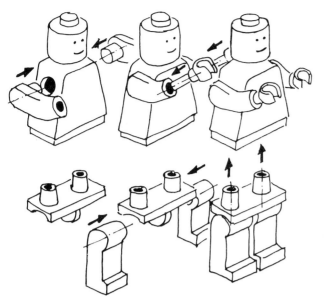

4

Assembly systems

SUMMARY

The concept of "assembly systems" covers labour force, machines and equipment. The task of the assembly system is to transform parts and components into a product. The most suitable type of assembly system will depend on the product's character and the complexity of assembly.

From the functional point of view an assembly system can be divided into a group of sub-systems – composing and handling systems for example. These sub-systems are recognisable in all assembly systems, irrespective of type although there will be variations in the equipment to be used, a handling system can for example be completely manual (little or no equipment) or completely automatic (conveyor belt, etc.).

It is necessary to differentiate between series-coupled, parallel-coupled and combined systems. Finally the chapter deals with a series of examples of characteristic assembly system designs.

Assembly systems

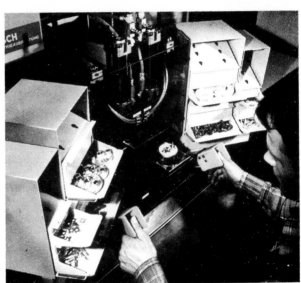

Fig. 4.1. Topmost from left:
- Puma robot welding car doors.
- Assembly line assembly at Danfoss Ltd.
- Hydro-electric generator at Hitachi.
- Mechanised assembly area (Bosch).
- Assembly machine for "Pipefix", (IPU for Broen Armature Ltd.).

4.1 Assembly systems

ASSEMBLY SYSTEM =
Operator/assembler
+
Machine/auxiliary
equipment

Assembly systems can be regarded as being composed of operator/assembler and machine/auxiliary equipment, regardless of the degree of mechanisation and automation. The assembly system itself is an organised unit geared to a goal but simultaneously acting as the integrated element in the total production apparatus.

An assembly system can be defined thus:

> AN ASSEMBLY SYSTEM is an integrated structure of machines and operators which achieves construction of subsystems or finished products with specific characteristics, using components or if necessary, formless materials (glue, etc.). This integration is achieved by using a process where the necessary operations are integrated in respect to material, energy and information.

Some types of assembly system:

A very broad spectrum of manual, mechanised and automated assembly systems exist in industry today. We will now briefly present some important definitions; these concepts will be examined in greater detail below.

Manual assembly: Assembly is carried out by the assembler who has simple and mostly passive auxiliary equipment at his disposal, such as tables, fixtures, component boxes, conveyor belt and hand tools.

Semi-automatic assembly: Automatic (programmed) machine system, where some operations are manual and adapted to the machine's program.

Automatic assembly: A machine system which follows a program. The system takes decisions on the basis of the program. Such decisions occur as the result of condition of the system and input, and realise the required output.

Flexible assembly: This is a system which allows for a variation of certain product characteristics.

Adaptive assembly: This in a system which adapts itself (automatically) to certain product variations (components) thus allowing a certain flexibility.

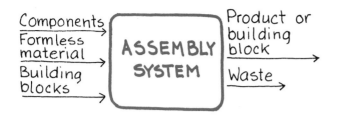

Assembly system's input/output

Machined parts and components are constructed into products in the assembly system. The material input can therefore range from components (parts, machined parts subassemblies) to formless material (glue, oil, paint) to building elements, i.e. large more complex product units. Output on the other hand can manifest itself in a finished building block that is to take its place later in a more complex product. A secondary output from the assembly system occurs occasionally in the form of waste (foil, clipping, magazines) or in the form of erroneously assembled products.

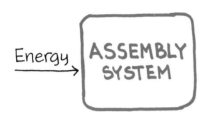

Energy is necessary to power mechanised assembly equipment, transport equipment as well as auxiliary equipment and includes lighting, heating and ventilation.

The assembly system can be divided into two control tasks:

– Technical control, meaning the systems determination or construction for execution of the required task.

– Organisational control, meaning the control of the assembly process in order to achieve the required productivity.

Information from assembly drawings, assembly instructions and parts lists will indentify the part used within the product and the numbers of each part that are required.

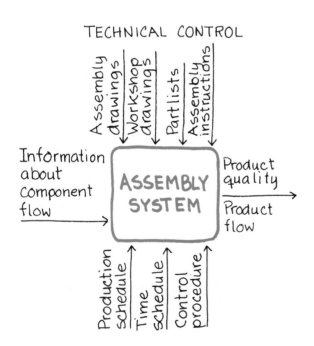

Production and time schedules in addition to controlling procedures shall ensure that the correct parts and components are available at the correct point in time and furthermore, that they are of the correct quality and quantity.

The input and output facets of the assembly system furnish information of present component flow and achieved production quality and quantity. This information is incorporated into the control of the subsequent production phase and also in reports on the total financial control.

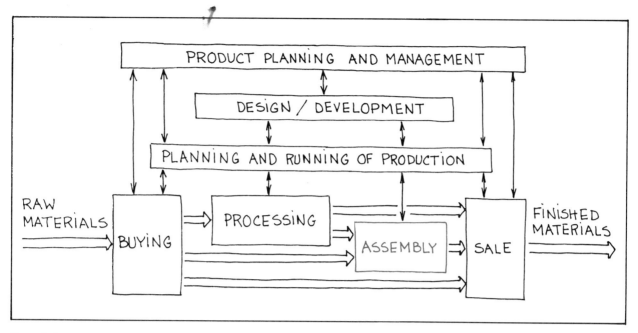

Fig. 4.2. System concept of a firm showing the relationship of assembly with the other functions (1).

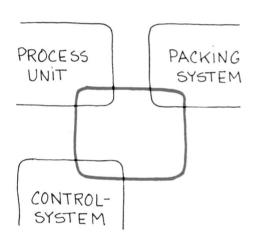

PROCESS UNIT

PACKING SYSTEM

CONTROL-SYSTEM

ASSEMBLY SYSTEM

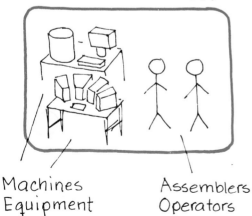

Machines Equipment

Assemblers Operators

The integration of the assembly system

In the technical concept of production (see Fig. 4.2) the assembly system is a separate unit which has relationships with buying, processing and sales and as well as to the production technique's preparation and control. One's concept of an assembly system today should be one of an integrated element, especially in connection with the processing area. Optimal determination of the assembly system can mean a non-optimal production system. The optimal solution could be a part or total integration of processing and assembly.

The content of the assembly system

The operators or assemblers who operate the machine equipment or carry out particular operations are included in the assembly system. The mechanical equipment which is part of the assembly system can be divided into three main groups:

★ Assembly equipment, e.g.

- Manual work area with table and boxes for parts and components. Hand tools and measuring equipment.
- Semi-automatic assembly machines or lines.
- Fully automatic assembly machines.

Subsystem of an assembly system

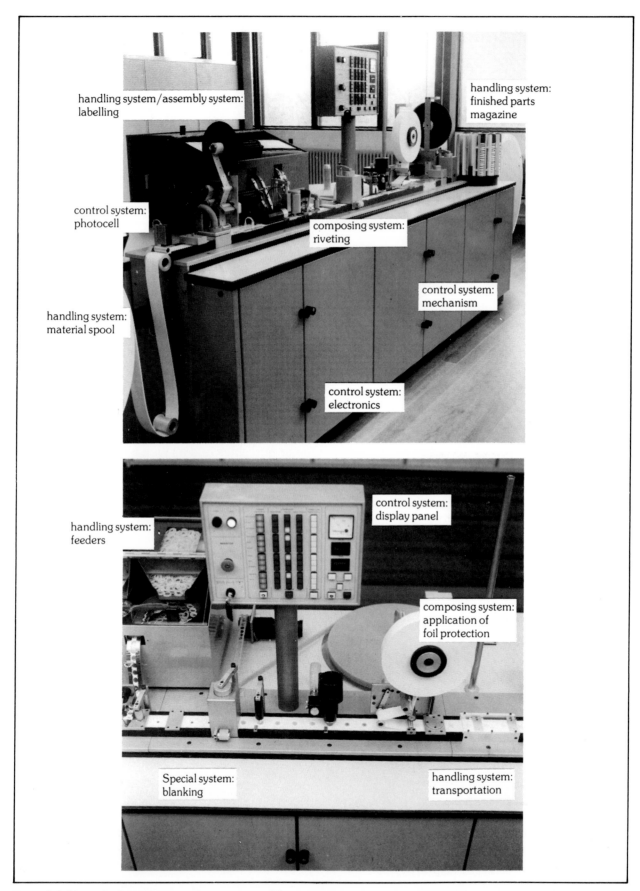

Fig. 4.3/4.4. Sub-systems of an assembly system, compare with description in Section 9.4. Assembly automat for ECG electrodes. (IPU for S & W).

★ Transport equipment
for transport of parts and components between assembly areas and from stores to assembly areas, i.e. conveyor belts, trucks, and chutes.

★ Buffers (buffer stores)
transport units where components can be in a waiting-position (magazines, conveyor or belts) or "passive" stores (boxes, magazines).

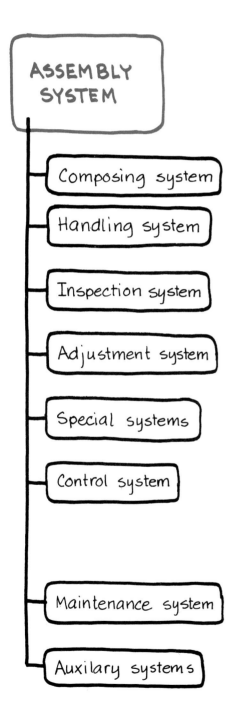

The assembly system's sub-systems

An assembly system can be divided up from the point of view of function. One or more sub-system tasks can be carried out by a single operator (certain handling, adjusting, controlling, inspection and maintenance).

★ The composing system's task is to join components.

★ The handling system's task is to store, transport and position components as well as tools and fixtures.

★ The inspection system shall control the quality and monitor the assembly system's functioning ability.

★ The adjustment system's task is to adjust positioning or composing of components.

★ The special systems are integrated sub-systems, e.g. processing or packaging systems.

★ The control system's tasks are twofold:
  – technical: the processing of information so the assembly process can be controlled.
  – organisational: processing of information that determines the rate of assembly and its placing in the production system.

★ The maintenance system's task is to prevent damage and aid alterations in the assembly system.

★ Auxiliary systems task can be to supply auxiliary material and energy.

4.2 The structure of assembly systems

The type and annual quantity of the product characterise the structure of the assembly system – in other words – the assembly system's complexity and degree of mechanisation and automation.

Depending on the task, the assembly system can be a combination of manual working stations and/or mechanical or automatic stations. These stations can be combined into a more or less automatic total system. The transport equipment will be an important part of such a total or complete system.

The assembly system could thus be envisaged in a two-dimensional grid as shown in Fig. 4.5, where the horizontal axis represents complexity and the vertical axis the degree of mechanisation and automation. The illustrated equipment examples can be characterised thus:

(a) Assembling automat constructed around a programmable handling unit. (Fully automatic).

(b) Automat with various operations, special machine (hard automation) with limited flexibility, fully automatic.

(c) Flexible assembly line with assembly units built from standard equipment. Fully automatic.

(d) Mechanised work area for a few assembly operations.

(e) Semi-automatic assembly equipment with manual and mechanised operations.

(f) Assembly line with manual and mechanised stations, semi-automatic, many operations.

(g) Manual assembly point.

(h) Amalgamation of various manual assembly points.

(i) Various manual assembly points amalgamated into a line layout, many operations.

Which system is to be chosen for a particular assembly task depends on a number of factors, primarily the product annual demand, size, complexity, required flexibility, in addition to the complexity of assembly and the capital available. We will come back to these points in Section 4.3 and Chapters 5 and 6.

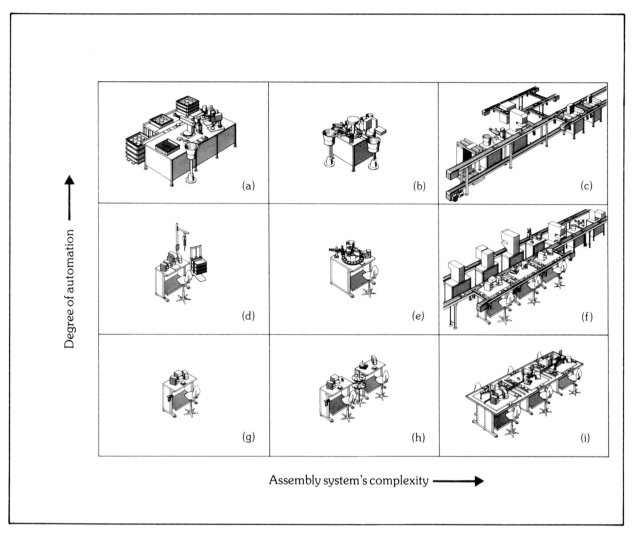

Fig. 4.5. Arrangement of assembly systems in a two dimensional grid according to complexity and degree of automation. (5).

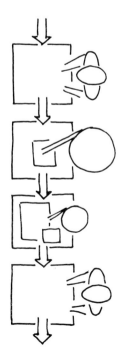

Series coupled assembly systems:

The individual stations are coupled in series, if the product under construction passes from one to the next in the assembly process. One or more components are assembled at every station. One can therefore refer to a simple flow of material through the system, which in turn eases material supply.

The cycle time in such a system is the sum of the longest operation and the transport time between two stations. The system can be exploited to the greatest possible extent when the operations are balanced so that each takes the same time. Manual series coupled systems, e.g. an assembly line, can be difficult to balance as work performance is individual and can vary during the course of a shift. One must normally accept a "loss of balance" of 5-15%, the loss being greatest in short cycle times.

From this point of view longer cycle times are desirable, though a demand for high production volume, i.e. short cycle time, undermines this.

Failure at any point in a series coupled system will mean a total stop. The probability that the complete system is running is the product of the individual station's efficiency.

$$D_{system} = D_1 \times D_2 \ldots D_n$$

If there are 10 stations each with a reliability of 0.97, the total system's reliability will be 0.74, in other words, it can be expected that the system will have a down time of 16%.

Manual series coupled assembly systems is often thought to be monotonous, with the operator tied to the assembly point and work methods are difficult to vary. The operator uses the same movements all the time in short cycle times which increases the risk of fatigue and boredom.

Working conditions and productivity can be improved by the use of buffers (buffer stores) between stations in these systems. The total reliability will be increased as a failure at one point does not mean the whole system stopping. Furthermore the operators can take short breaks or help at one of the other stations.

IBM in Amsterdam is a good example of the use of buffers in a series coupled assembly system.

Here one had very positive experience of the use of "minilines" in typewriter assembly. Originally one had 2 lines with 60 operators in each, constructed without buffers and having a cycle time of 3 minutes, with typical problems on a widespread scale. Later assembly was transformed to "minilines" of 18 operators and a cycle time of about 10 minutes. The layout of this system is shown in Fig. 4.6. The M-construction increases the possibilities for communication among the operators.

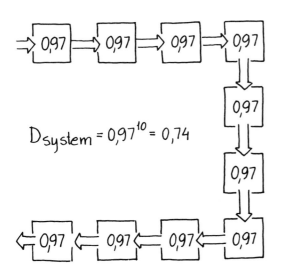

$$D_{system} = 0.97^{10} = 0.74$$

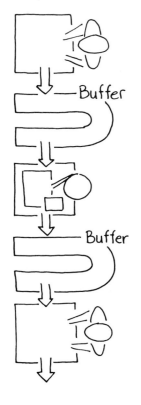

Buffer

Buffer

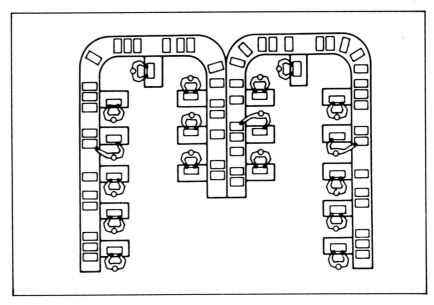

Fig. 4.6. Miniline with buffer stores (in transport system) for assembly of typewriters (6).

Parallel coupled assembly systems:

The individual stations or work areas are coupled in parallel when the same assembly operation is carried out at various points in the system. Material supply is complicated in such systems as all components must be distributed to all stations; consequently assembly equipment must be available in many places.

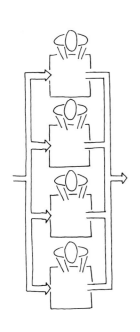

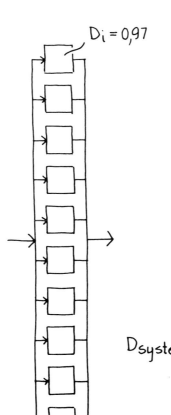

$D_i = 0,97$

The cycle time for a parallel coupled system is the sum of the cycle time for one of the stations plus any transport time. Balancing is composed only of the adjustment of the number of parallels to satisfy the required volume of production. The probability of such a system functioning can be expressed as the probability of all stations not working simultaneously:

$$D_{system} = 1 - (1-D_1)(1-D_2)\ldots(1-D_n)$$

With a parallel coupled system of 10 stations, each with a function probability of 0.97, the total system function efficiency will be very nearly 1.

$$D_{system} = 1 - (1-0,97)^{10} \approx 1$$

In such a system the operator is not bound to the same extent as in a series-coupled system. The parallel system does not require every point to be manned in order to function, resulting in greater flexibility in the case of breaks and absence.

Combined systems

In practice assembly systems are often a combination of both parallel and series coupled systems. Thus material supply is simplified, less assembly equipment is required and the operator enjoys a freer work situation. Examples are illustrated beneath.

Connection with the products structures

Only with 100% manually assembled products does one enjoy full freedom to choose the structure of the assembly system. In other cases the products design is decisive in establishing the optimal system structure. This is emphasised in Chapters 6 and 7 where the connection between assembly methods and product structure is dealt with.

Flexibility

Flexibility is not a precise concept. Generally it means: "the ability to change or transform", either passively or actively. A system's flexibility is a structural characteristic and can therefore be "read" from its physical design. The concept "flexibility" should not be used without qualifying what it applies to.

Flexibility can be conceived as:

★   A production system's ability to carry out tasks without large adjustments. (Versatility).

★ A production system's ability to adapt to new demands from production tasks without the required tools permanently being available. (Adaptability).

★ Independence in the choice of various modes of processing for various production tasks in multi-station systems. (Passage flexibility).

★ Presence of more than the required function units, which can be used in an emergency. (Production redundancy).

★ A production system's ability to expand in order to increase quantitative capacity. (Quantitative expansion possibility).

★ A production system's ability to expand in order to increase qualitative capacity. (Qualitative expansion possibility).

★ Possibility for balancing out of different work times in work stations that follow each other directly.

The designations in brackets should be regarded as being more precise than the concepts.

Flexibility is generally a useful system characteristic, in other words it can be of importance to choose assembly systems containing a high degree of flexibility. Flexibility's outer limits are the purely manual systems. Fig. 4.7 shows the relation between machine and operator flexibility.

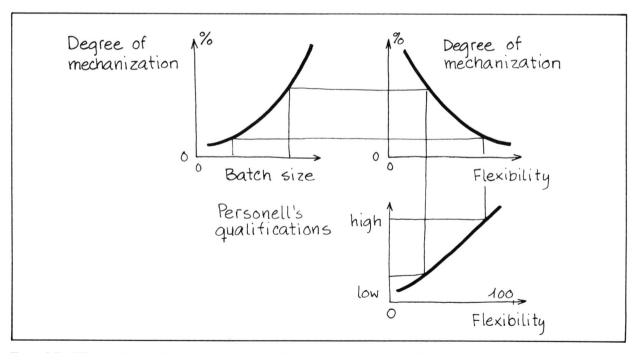

Fig. 4.7. The relationship between machine and operator flexibility. The curves show the technique's state: large batch sizes mean high degree of mechanisation, thereby low machine flexibility and low operator flexibility. (7).

4.3 Assembly system's characteristics

We will now enlarge upon the product's connection with the type of assembly system. We will deal with complexity, assembly time and annual demand in order to characterise the product.

The following divisions can be applied to the size of production and its distribution.

★   Single or limited assembly: 1-5 examples per year, e.g. moulds, prototypes.

★   Series assembly: non-continuous assembly of more than five examples per year, e.g. special tools, larger electric motors, machines tools.

★   Continuous assembly: assembly of a product and its eventual variants throughout the year, e.g. carpet sweepers, ovens, private cars.

Both the product's complexity (its composition) and its complication (its degree of difficulty) play a part in the assembly system. A principle division follows: (no distinction here between complexity and complication):

★   Non-complex products: simple planning, production and assembly, e.g. standard tools, simple machine elements.

★   Medium complex products: reasonably difficult planning, production or assembly, e.g. pumps, power drills, household apparatus.

★   Complicated products: difficult planning, production or assembly: e.g. NC machines, complicated measuring instruments, copying machines, TV, cars.

The product's assembly time also plays a part in the choice of assembly system. An important limit lies at 30 minutes:

★   Short assembly time: assembly time under 30 minutes, e.g. standard tools, hand drills, carpet sweepers.

★   Long assembly time: assembly time over 30 minutes, e.g. tool machines, cars, specialised measuring instruments.

Classification of assemblies

Assembly can be classified as above, based on complexity, assembly time and size of production. We will refer to this classification of assembly systems in the following section.

4.4 Examples of assembly systems

Below and on the following pages we have illustrated some characteristic assembly systems which cover some of the alternatives (automatic and mechanised) described in Fig. 4.5.

Commentary of some typical products for each of the examples will be made.

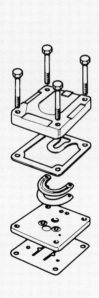
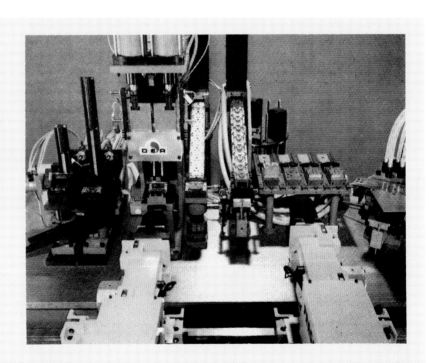

Flexible assembly automat. Constructed for non-complex and medium complex products in series and variant assembly. The illustration shows an arrangement with Pragma A3000 assembly robots from D.E.A. (Italy). The arrangement is for the assembly of compressor valves with 12 components. When the required production quantity has been reached the tools are changed and the robot reprogrammed for other assembly operations. Such assembly systems are expected to be widespread *in the future*, but may be said to lack the requisite development at the present time in order to be used in normal production.

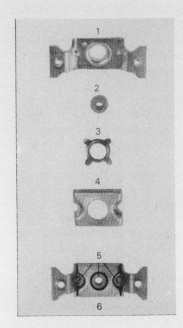 

Rotary index machine for fully automatic assembly of bearing caps (5 components) for small electric motors. Cycle time about 2.5 seconds. (Montech AG, Switzerland).

Rotary index machines are used typically for non-complex products (with few components) in continuous assembly.

Machine for valve assembly, constructed with 3 separate stations with buffers in between. Cycle time about 2.5 seconds. See also example on pages 36-37 (IPU for Kosan Teknova Ltd).

Machines of this type are used for both non-complex and medium complex products in continuous assembly.

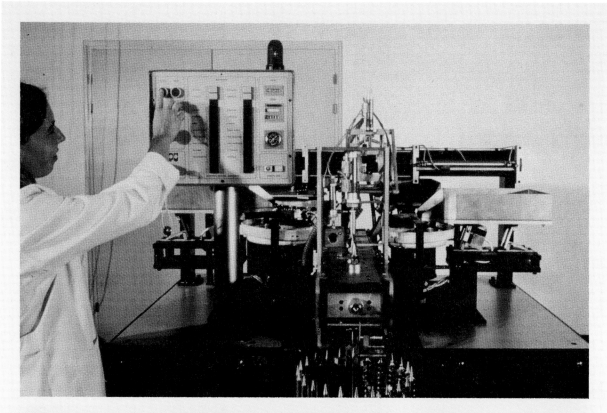

Machine constructed with indexing line layout. There is a rigid coupling between the various stations as in the case of rotary index machines. Both types therefore are only suitable to non-complex products in continuous assembly. The machine illustrated was constructed by IPU for Broen Armature Ltd. Cycle time about 2.5 seconds. The machine is fully automatic (assembly) but packaging is undertaken manually, in that the operator takes the products already assembled from the rotary table at the front of the machine.

Assembly line constructed of standard equipment for Lanco Economic. The illustrated line assembles quartz alarm clocks (41 components) fully automatically. Cycle time is about 4 seconds.

Systems of this type are used for medium complex products in continuous assembly.

Sub assembly and components for quartz alarm clocks.

Unmechanised work point (BOSCH).

This type is used for non-complex, medium complex and complex products in batch assembly.

Semi-automatic assembly machine for door handles. (C & J Machines Ltd). Well suited to non-complex products in continuous assembly, in other words it covers about the same area as the fully automatic counterpart but normally with a longer cycle time. On the other hand it can save a lot of money as the operator carries out the tasks which would be difficult and expensive to carry out fully automatically.

63

Semi-automatic assembly line with both manual and automatic operations (BOSCH). There are buffer stores between the manual and automatic stations, so that the operator is not tied to the machine's cycle.

This type is used for medium complex products in series and continuous assembly.

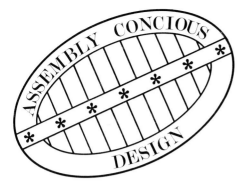

What is – Design for ease of assembly?

SUMMARY

A rationalisation of assembly comprises an improvement in the effectiveness of assembly, the quality of the product and the assembly system's environment.

Easily the most effective opportunities for rationalisation lie in the product's design phase as it is here that assembly is determined.

The product's designer must therefore be able to envisage the consequences of his decisions and the effects they will have on product assembly:

- he must know which design parameters decide the quality of assembly (in a broad sense)

- he must design the product to achieve high quality

- he must be aware of the general principles of design for ease of assembly in order to tackle the very complicated task which faces him.

This chapter deals with complex optimisation tasks. The following chapters deal with possibilities for rationalisation in the realm of product policy, product assortment and product structure and component level.

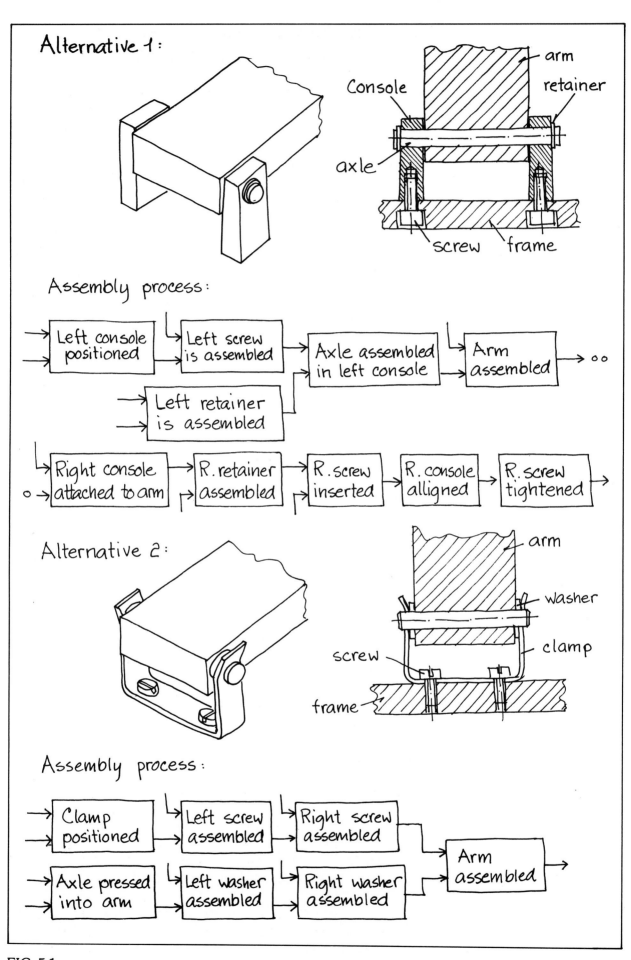

FIG. 5.1.

5.1 Design for ease of assembly – rationalising assembly

Assembly rationalisation can, as mentioned in Chapter 1, be applied in many areas, not least in the process of production but also as the designer decides on and fixes assembly almost totally, in the design phase. The key to a thorough rationalisation therefore is to be found here.

The task of rationalisation therefore must be looked upon as *total*, in other words as an optimisation of the whole product and production system. Section 5.3 deals with some of the many factors which are part of this complex optimisation. There are four main goals which must be emphasised:

– improvement of the effectiveness of assembly, i.e. increased productivity in relation to manpower and investment resources.

– improvement of product quality – i.e. improved product value from the buyer's standpoint in relation to the product's price.

– improvement of the assembly system's profitability, i.e. increased utilisation of equipment.

– improvement of working environment within the assembly system.

Production systems are normally conservative: changes in product or system create both foreseeable and unforeseeable problems – and therefore should be avoided. A reorganisation of assembly should not be regarded as an end in itself but should be used as a link in a total rationalisation using the four goals mentioned above.

Design rationalisation

The designer determines the structure of the product, i.e. its component construction and the mode in which these components are joined (assembly) in addition to determining the design of components. This will normally result in a fairly precise production process and a correspondingly precise assembly process. If the designer proposes alternative production structure the number and type of processes and assemblies will be altered; if he proposes a different component design still other process and assembly methods will have to be applied, see Fig. 5.1.

The most radical assembly improvements lie in selecting and designing product alternatives in which certain assemblies can be disposed of or greatly simplified, in other words:

> Assembly can first and foremost be rationalised by changing the product so that assembly becomes superfluous or at least, simplified.

Production oriented rationalisation

If we assume the starting point is in the production apparatus, particularly in the assembly system then opportunities for rationalisation lie in exploiting an optimal assembly system.

In his design of the product, the designer determines which type of assembly system is feasible, in addition to establishing how the system will function through his specification of the components' quality. He will, simultaneously with these tasks, decide the basis of the assembly processes mechanisation and automation which determines the products that can be assembled on this assembly equipment. We will examine this in greater detail.

A product cannot be regarded in isolation when we are discussing assembly problematics. A product is normally divided into a series of product variants; certain sub-systems in the product can appear in other products and certain components can be applied in various sub-systems or can be produced because of group-technological similarities with other components.

Thus, design for ease of assembly can be said to be the process of achieving the insertion of a single product into a well-structured product, building element and component program.

5.2 When can design for ease of assembly be applied?

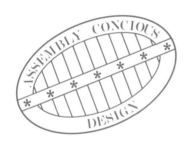

The answer is not "always". The designer will normally concentrate first and foremost on getting the product to function within the economic limitations laid down. Time is at a premium; as a result the most important activity in the closing phase of design is to get the product detailed so it can be in production as soon as possible, in other words getting the drawing finished. Assembly deliberations can easily becaome a minor part of a large hectic process – the result being a non-optimal product from the assembly point of view.

Various modes of operation

Products resulting from optimal assembly are developed today by means of a design process consisting of many steps. The finished marketed product is given a quality "lift" by means of an extra effort, focusing on assembly, although one will try to implement the advantages of experience already gained while making this effort. Consequently the *design degrees of freedom* are of limited application in the assembly effort. As we shall see in later chapters the creation of such degrees of freedom play an important part in the attainment of good assembly results.

An alternative – better but seldom used – mode of operation is to attach greater significance to assembly deliberations in the early phases of design, in order that the total product's structure and design is geared to an optimal assembly process. Such a process will normally require parallel development of product and production system, with special emphasis on the assembly system, hereby created the title "integrated product development", which is dealt with in Chapter 9.

Whilst it should be possible to take account of assembly during a normal design project, the task is extremely complex and demands that either the designer is particularly conscious of assembly problems, or that the design team includes members with particular knowledge of the area.

Design for ease of assembly requires expert knowledge of the following:

- ★ Joining methods and processes

- ★ The connection between product design and assembly process.

- ★ The connection between product design and the type and quality of assembly systems.

5.3 What is an optimal result?

One can contend that the purchaser is not prepared to pay anything for assembly. Assembly is only a means of achieving coherence in the product and not of contributing to saleable quality. When looked at from this angle it becomes obvious that criteria necessary for an optimal assembly (i.e. low production and assembly costs) must be tempered by the allowable overhead costs to achieve them. Further these desirable criteria should not adversely effect other criteria such as good design, long life and functionability.

A thorough rationalisation of assembly starting with design alterations can have much greater consequences, particularly the extent of its value to a firm, as illustrated in Fig. 5.2. The points in the figure can be regarded as vital criteria in the choice of assembly technology and show that the criteria will vary greatly:

- ★ Technological criteria

- ★ Financial criteria

- ★ Organisational criteria

- ★ Personnel-related criteria

This indicates that the assembly system is an element of or is closely connected to the production system, the firm's organisation, economic management and personnel, including the individual operator/assembler.

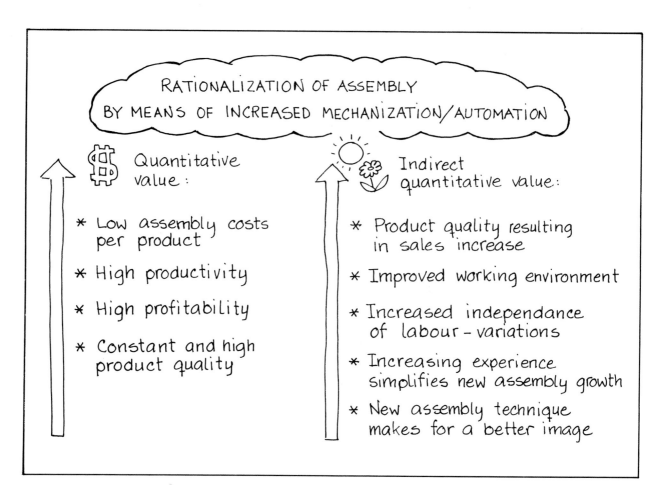

Fig. 5.2. Survey of parameters which can play a part in a firm's assessment of the positive facets of the execution of an automation project. ([8]).

It is the designer's task to choose, specify and develop assembly methods (expressed in the product's structure and design) which promote an improvement of the following superior criteria:

    ★   Constant high product quality

    ★   High productivity

    ★   High profitability

    ★   Good working environment

Such improvements are naturally first and foremost the responsibility of the production manager, who designs and develops the assembly equipment, while the product's designer determines the basic practicability and the technical level of assembly rationalisation.

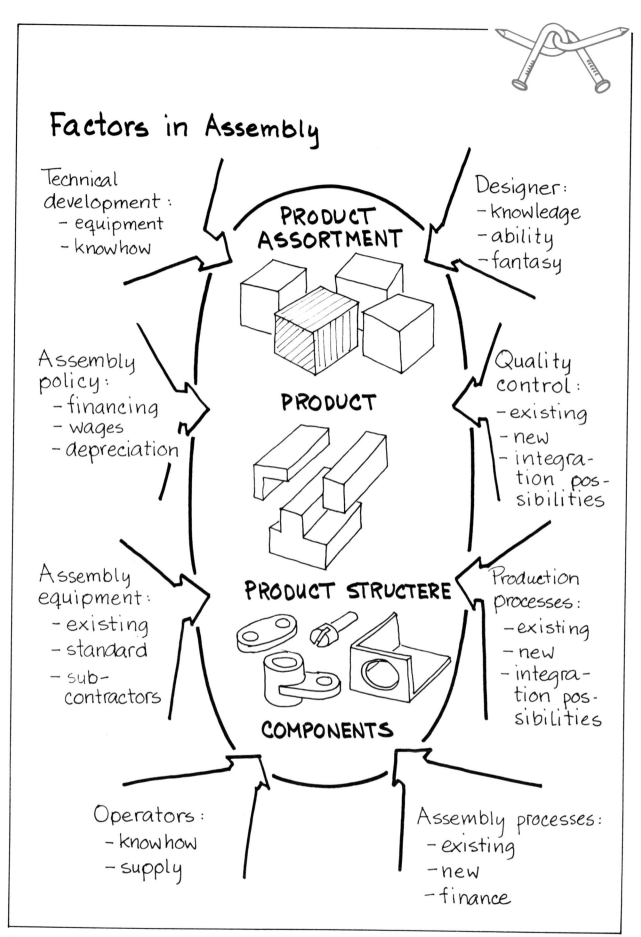

Factors in Assembly

Technical development:
- equipment
- knowhow

Designer:
- knowledge
- ability
- fantasy

PRODUCT ASSORTMENT

Assembly policy:
- financing
- wages
- depreciation

PRODUCT

Quality control:
- existing
- new
- integration possibilities

Assembly equipment:
- existing
- standard
- subcontractors

PRODUCT STRUCTERE

Production processes:
- existing
- new
- integration possibilities

COMPONENTS

Operators:
- knowhow
- supply

Assembly processes:
- existing
- new
- finance

Fig. 5.3. Survey of important factors with influence on the design process (determination of product assortment, product structure and components).

5.4 Three areas of application

A constructive application with a view to rationalisation of assembly can be applied to three areas or on three levels:

Chapter 6 ⟵   ★   Product assortment

Chapter 7 ⟵   ★   Product (structure, building blocks)

Chapter 8 ⟵   ★   Components

Such application, whether it be purely revision of a product or a new design, can occur in the following ways:

   ★   Creation of design degrees of freedom, so that alternatives containing good assembly-oriented characteristics can be created.

   ★   Application of the principles of design for ease of assembly, primarily elimination and secondly principles of improvement.

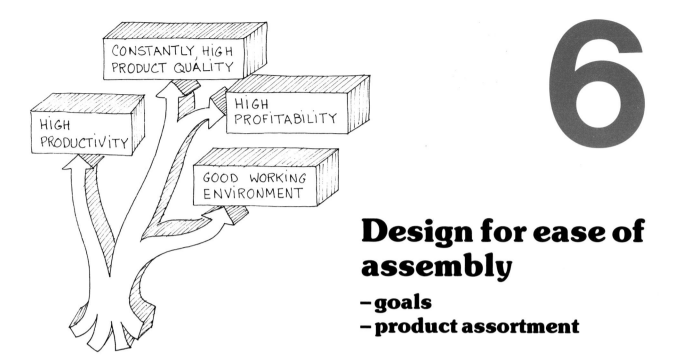

Design for ease of assembly
– goals
– product assortment

SUMMARY

A series of decisions which exert considerable influence on the feasibility of rationalising a product's assembly, are taken during the design phase. It is therefore important for the designer to bear the principles of design for ease of assembly in mind.

In optimising assembly an optimisation of the following criteria is striven for: high product quality, high profitability and a good working environment. A group of general principles and guide lines apply to each of these criteria.

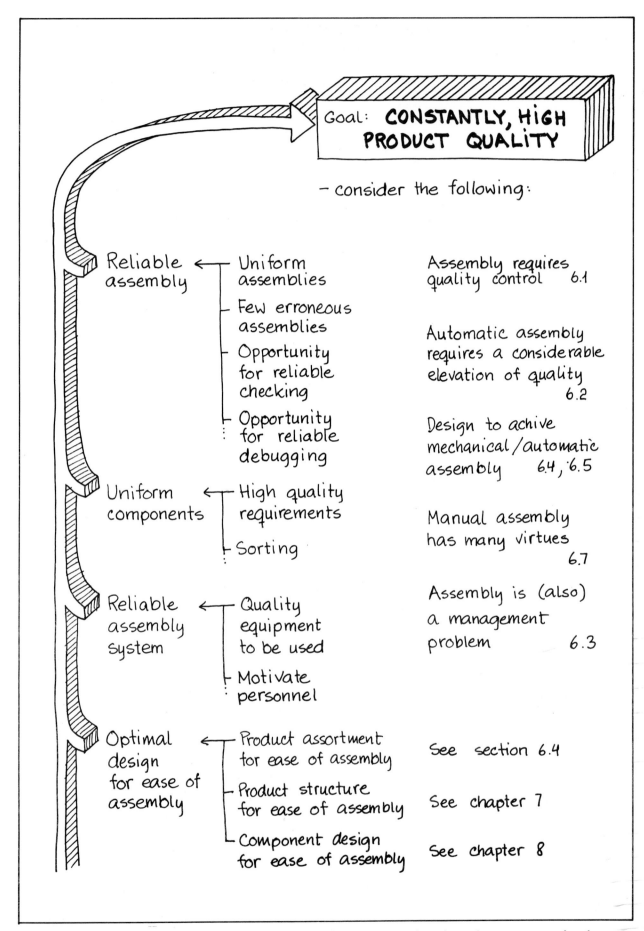

Fig. 6.1. Principles and assumptions which should be considered in the process of achieving CONSTANTLY HIGH PRODUCT QUALITY.

6.1 Criteria for optimal assembly

In this chapter we will tackle assembly problematics at the earliest stage of the design phase, namely the stage at which a new product development project is determined, where the problem is defined. At this stage it will be possible to take decisions which can *radically* affect the rationalisation of assembly.

The general goal of optimal assembly can be divided into factors, each of which contribute to the achievement of that goal. Every one of these factors can be observed in the light of various principles and means of design which can in turn be regarded as *principles of design for (ease of) assembly*.

The following section deals with those factors which contribute to optimal assembly as well as those design steps which lead up to it. These steps can be formulated as principles or guidelines which normally lead to a positive result.

As stated in Chapter 5 optimal assembly can be regarded as an optimisation of the following criteria:

* ★ Constant, high product quality
* ★ High productivity
* ★ High profitability
* ★ Good working environment

6.2 Achieving HIGH PRODUCT QUALITY

In Fig. 6.1 this goal is seen in relation to the factors which contribute to its achievement and the design steps and principles which subscribe to the same goal.

Optimal assembly-orientated design is the "alpha and omega" of product quality. A long series of principles can be applied, partly on the level of product assortment (this chapter), partly on that of product structure (Chapter 7) and finally on component level (Chapter 8).

The reliability of the assembly process depends on the operations, components and equipment – personnel being included in the last category. There are, as illustrated in Fig. 6.1, some general principles which can contribute to a reliable assembly process; these will be described and examined on the following pages.

Mechanised assembly, and to an even greater extent, automated assembly, extremely sensitive to alterations and variations in the characteristics or quality of components.

Testing and checking of components and sub-systems is a problem which must be included at an early stage of the deliberations on product structuring. The product's division into building blocks (see also Section 7.4) can in some cases be dictated by the particular philosophy of testing which is applied.

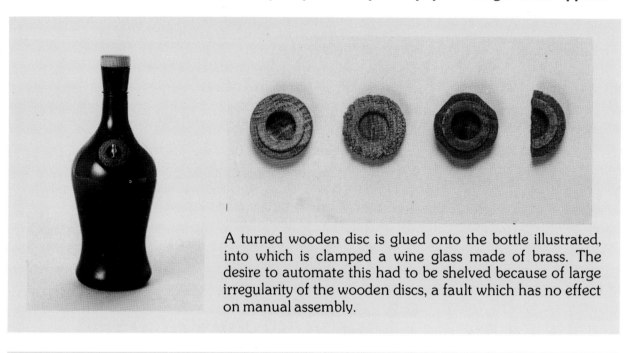

A turned wooden disc is glued onto the bottle illustrated, into which is clamped a wine glass made of brass. The desire to automate this had to be shelved because of large irregularity of the wooden discs, a fault which has no effect on manual assembly.

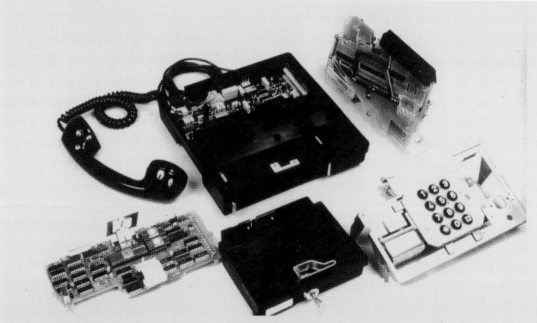

GNT Automatic's coin telephone is constructed of building blocks which can be assembled parallel and quality-controlled individually before the final assembly phase.

The automatic equipment's tools normally demand a much narrower limit of tolerance than those necessary for manual or mechanised assembly. Sometimes these tolerance requirements must be applied to non-functional dimensions purely out of consideration to assembly. The reason for this is that the equipment's fixtures, tools, channels, etc. also have tolerances and consequently cannot allow for large component variation in those components taking part in the assembly process.

These increased quality demands on components will normally lead to a general improvement in product quality when one switches over to automatic assembly.

Areas of tolerance for various modes of assembly. Note that automatic assembly demands narrow tolerances. (9).

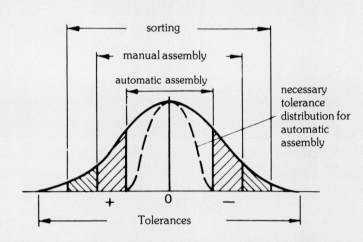

This plastic ring for use in ECG electrodes (see pages 80 and 139 as well as Section 9.4) requires only loose tolerances in order to function according to requirements in the electrode.

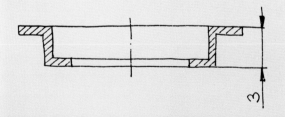

Functional tolerance ± 0.2.

Tolerance due to
the assembly equipment ± 0.1.

But tighter tolerances on the ring are required in regard to the assembly equipment especially the feeding and handling equipment.

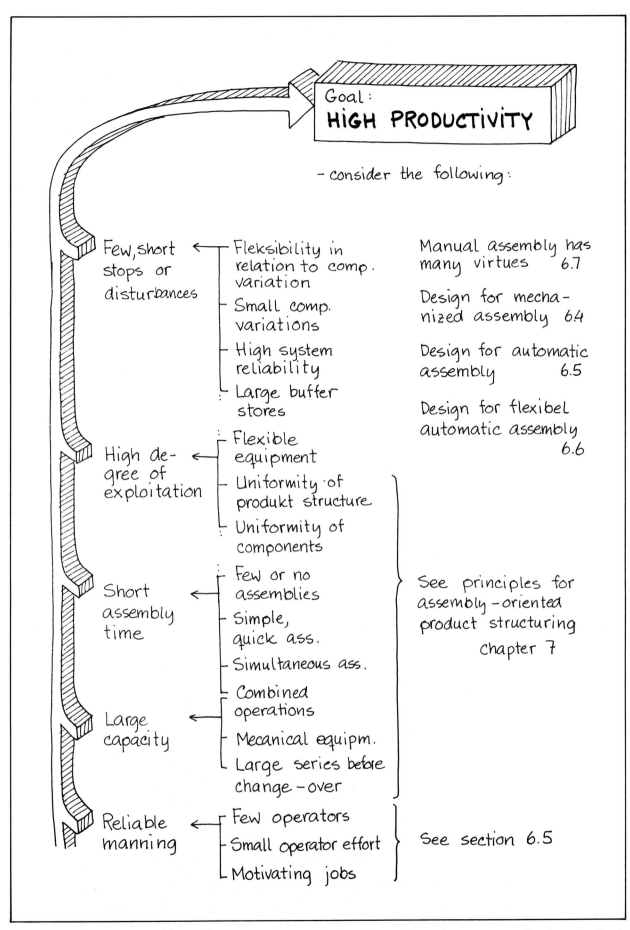

Fig. 6.2. Principles and hypotheses which should be considered in the process of achieving high productivity.

The transformation to more rational assembly, be it mechanised, semi-automatic or fully automatic assembly equipment is an activity which can only be achieved optimally by means of an *integrated* effort, i.e. an effort in the realms of product planning, design, quality control, preparation and production.

This principle is examined in greater detail in Chapter 9.

6.3 Attainment of HIGH PRODUCTIVITY

We will here, as in Section 6.2, examine the factors, design efforts and principles which contribute to the establishment of the good "high productivity", see Fig. 6.2. We have chosen to formulate principles which relate to the degrees of mechanisation and automation of the assembly system.

Design for mechanised assembly   (Principle 6.4)

in order to achieve:
- uniform assemblies
- few erroneous assemblies
- uniform high quality
- great system reliability
- large capacity
- reliable manning

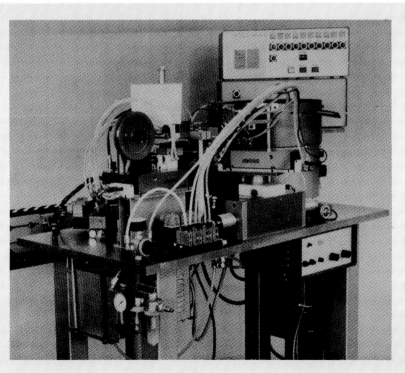

Two platinum filaments are welded together in this automat (Fa. Micro-technik), the breaking strain in the joint is tested and the filament laid in a bent quartz tube (24 joints/min). It would hardly have been possible to produce this product with uniform quality without mechanisation.

in order to achieve:
– uniform assemblies
– few erroneous assemblies
– uniform high quality
– great system reliability
– reliable operator effort
– motivating jobs

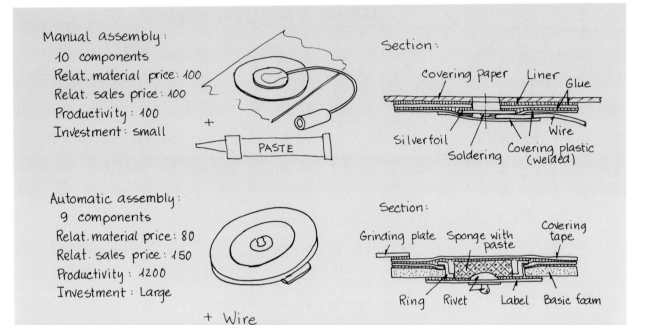

Manual assembly:
  10 components
  Relat. material price: 100
  Relat. sales price: 100
  Productivity: 100
  Investment: small
  + PASTE

Section:
  Covering paper   Liner   Glue
  Silverfoil   Soldering   Covering plastic (welded)   Wire

Automatic assembly:
  9 components
  Relat. material price: 80
  Relat. sales price: 150
  Productivity: 1200
  Investment: Large
  + Wire

Section:
  Grinding plate   Sponge with paste   Covering tape
  Ring   Rivet   Label   Basic foam

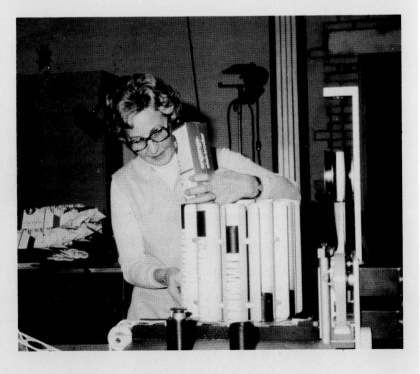

Two variations of the ECG electrode. B is designed for automatic assembly. This example is dealt with in detail in Chapter 9: Integrated product development. (Design of electrode and production apparatus: IPU for S & W).

in order to achieve:
- the same advantages as with automatic assembly in addition to:
- flexibility in relation to component variation ("coincidental")
- flexibility in relation to component variation ("planned")
- flexibility in relation to product variation ("planned")

Power switch in 4 variations (LK-NES). These 4 are assembled in the same automated assembly machine.

Indicator instruments for cars can be cited as a large example of a product which is designed for flexible automatic assembly. These are produced by Nippondenso Co. Ltd., Japan, up to 400,000-500,000 per month and in roughly 150 variants.

The instruments, which all function according to the same principle are used as fuel gauges, temperature gauges and oil pressure gauges in various car models.

By designing for flexible automatic assembly it was possible to standardise the individual components so that all variants could be assembled automatically.

Each component-type is now produced in the form of maximum 4 variants, as opposed to 20 before standardisation. It is mathematically possible to produce 288 different indicator instruments using the selected component design, in practice, however, only about 150 are used.

The assembly system for these instruments is constructed in the form of a series of individual stations with buffer stores (conveyor belt catering for max. 40 units) between each station.

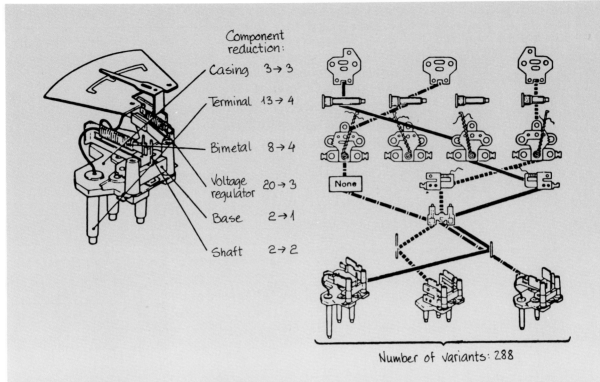

Component reduction:

Casing   3 → 3
Terminal   13 → 4
Bimetal   8 → 4
Voltage regulator   20 → 3
Base   2 → 1
Shaft   2 → 2

None

Number of variants: 288

The system's cycle time is roughly 1 sec., and the change between the variants is accomplished in the same time. It is therefore financially justifiable to produce the variants in series from 40 pieces upwards. Production is not normally for temporary stores. The number of instruments produced is geared to each clients daily needs and the type of car that client assembles.

The instrument's type number and numbers for the respective orders are typed into the control system together with the order sequence. A flow checking unit identifies the instruments in production and monitors the operations at each station. The automatic conversion of each station is carried out in the following way.

A dummy (special component) is sent down the line between adjacent orders. This is detected by a receiver at each station it passes, which reports that the variant is to be changed. The particular station checks back to the general control system about which type is now to be produced. Information on number of units required is only supplied to the first station, the following stations will continue to produce until the next dummy appears. At each station a simple mechanical handling equipment will take a component, assemble it, check the resulting assembly and send the partly-assembled instrument on to the next station.

The assembly system's main data:

1. Maximum monthly production, 500,000 instruments
2. Cycle time: 1 sec.
3. No. of product variants: 150
4. Conversion time to new variant: 1 sec.
5. No. of conversions: typically 200 pieces/day
6. Minimum production size: 1 (in normal production series however, at least 40)

among others:
- great flexibility towards:
    - various product types
    - product variants
    - component variation
    - faulty components
    - unforeseen assembly problems
- low investment in equipment
- greater job satisfaction(than with mech./aut. assembly).

Mechanical/automatic assembly is not a universal solution to problems of overheads and expense. The human being is vastly superior to the machine in many respects, first and foremost concerning flexibility. Manual assembly is best therefore, when conversion ability is required, either because of frequently changing tasks or by reason of their complexity.

Manual piano assembly (Yamaha). Such an assembly would probably be impossible to automate.

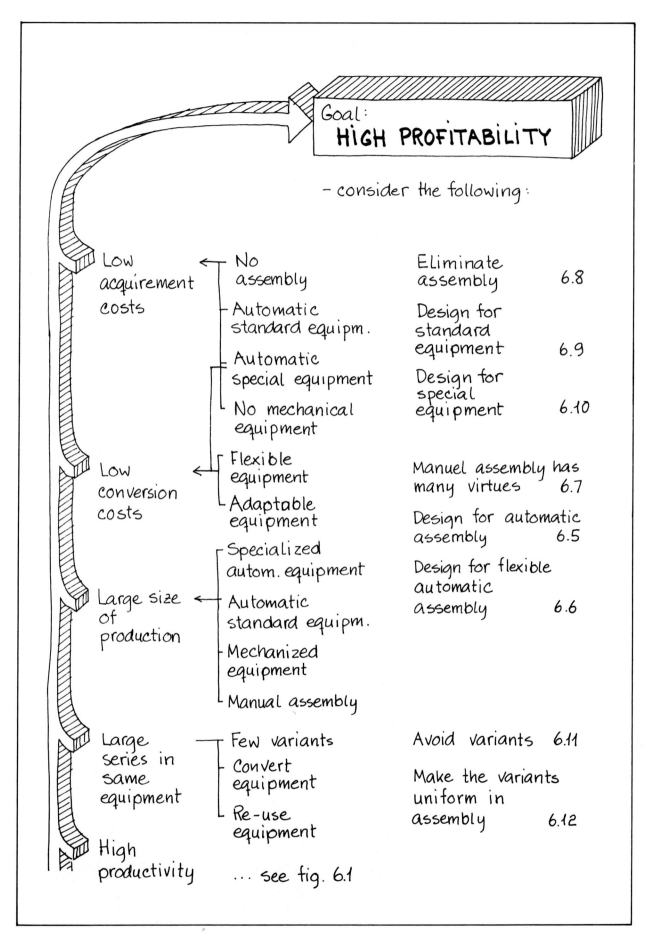

Fig. 6.3. Principles and hypotheses to be considered in the process of achieving HIGH PROFITABILITY.

6.4 Attainment of HIGH PROFITABILITY

Profitability in this context should be perceived as yield or savings in relation to investment in a particular product's assembly. The profitability will be high if the investment is small or the savings great. But if the equipment's application is extended to the product's variants or to all products possibly including a suitable conversion effort, the equipment's profitability will be increased even more.

The designer can, as shown in Fig. 6.3, influence profitability in a variety of ways. The principles mentioned will now be dealt with.

| | Eliminate assembly | (Principle 6.8) |

in order to achieve:
– a thorough reduction of assembly costs.

The designer is, as mentioned in Chapter 5, all-powerful in respect of the product's structure and therefore the extent of assembly. If he can hit upon well-suited production processes, components and suitable product structure, assembly can be minimised or even eliminated.

Chapter 7 deals with assembly from the point of view of process deliberation. In this section we will examine closer the possibilities which lie in product structuring and in the choice of part-products and components.

This frame for the motor in a household electricity meter from LK-NES is built from punched and bent sheet metal parts, which are welded together and finally surface treated. In the alternative design the functional surfaces are obtained by using a pressure moulding of zinc alloy.

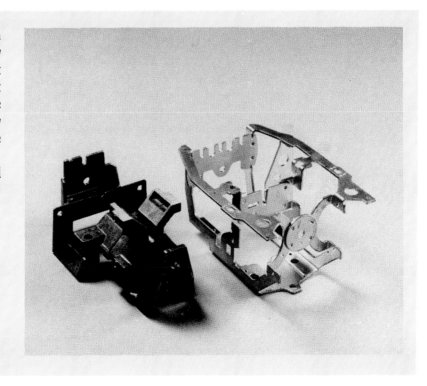

in order to:
- exploit marketed mass-produced equipment to a relatively low price
- exploit well-tried principles and equipment
- exploit equipment which can be adapted to other tasks

Some examples of standard equipment are shown below. In Chapter 8 we will deal with the design principles which apply to the product components adaptation to various types of standard equipment.

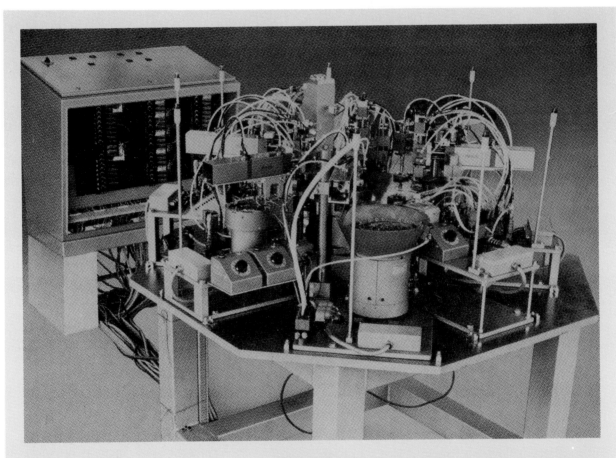

This automat assembles potentiometers. It is constructed from standard electric and pneumatic equipment from fa. Microtechnik.

The components illustrated are assembled in 2.3 seconds.

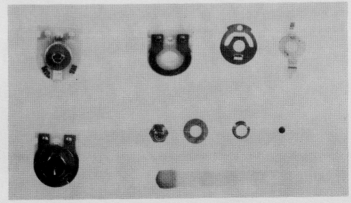

in order to:
- be able to take advantage of processes or assembly operations which can not be realised manually or with normal mechanical equipment
- achieve high integration, e.g. between production and assembly processes
- achieve optimal harmony between machine and size of production.

These days the border line between standard and special equipment is blurred with more and more tasks being carried out with standard equipment.

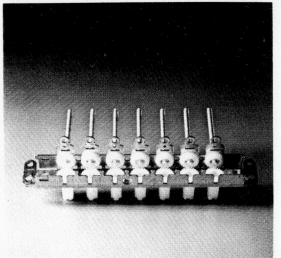

This drive for diode tuning is cast as an integral part of a steel plate, after which it is bent so that the gears can engage. (See also page 110). (Hoechst).

in order to:
- be able to assemble larger quantitites on the same equipment.

Variants should not only be regarded as product variants, but also those of sub-systems, building blocks and components. The number of variants plays an important part during dimensioning of the assembly equipment. Fig. 6.4 illustrates various structurings of assembly equipment having taken account of variants:

- building blocks which are used in various products can, if uniform, be assembled on common equipment.

- if the variants are designed so that variant features appear as far up the assembly chain as possible, then the majority of the equipment can be common (Principle 6.12).

- if one wishes to assemble many variants on the same equipment then great demands will be made on that equipment's flexibility.

The type of equipment used will depend on the flexibility requirements. Very often the final, variant-creating assembly task is undertaken manually in order to take advantage of the assembler's flexibility and checking abilities.

The principle of avoiding variants contributes therefore to a simplification of the assembly structure in Fig. 6.4.

These fittings for air hoses are a typical example of principle 6.12. One has achieved the assembly on the same assembly equipment of the two variations (for 3mm and 4mm diameter hoses), without actual conversion. This as a result of the selected design. (Festo Pneumatics).

so that:
- one can increase the size of production in the assembly system
- one can lessen instructions, conversions, the number of components, etc. in the assembly system

An explanation of the principle's importance is given above. Chapter 7 deals with various principles of variant creation.

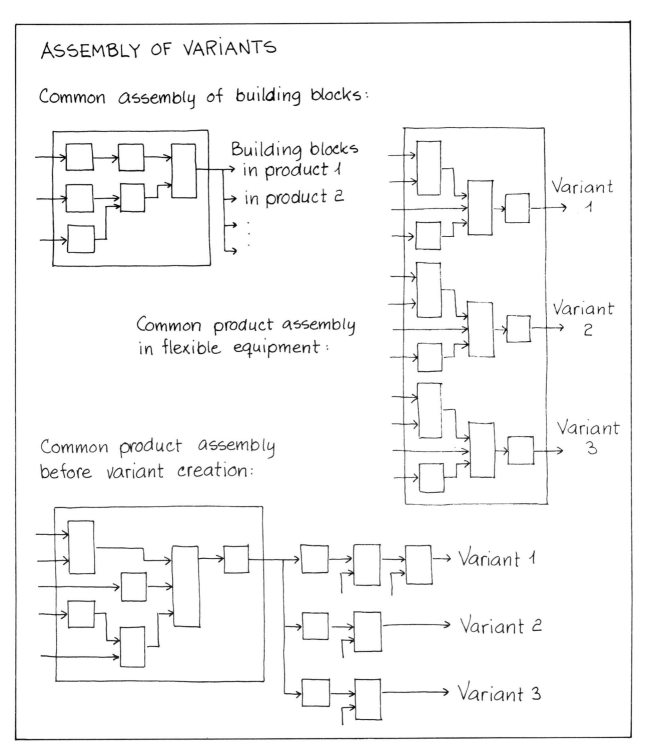

ASSEMBLY OF VARIANTS

Common assembly of building blocks:

Building blocks
→ in product 1
→ in product 2

→ Variant 1

Common product assembly in flexible equipment:

→ Variant 2

→ Variant 3

Common product assembly before variant creation:

→ Variant 1
→ Variant 2
→ Variant 3

Fig. 6.4. Connection between product assortment and assembly structure.

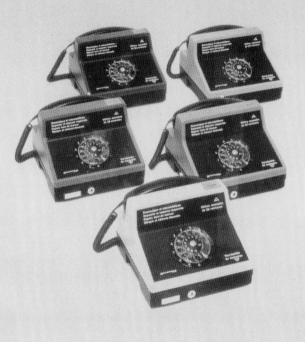

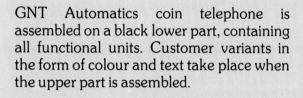

GNT Automatics coin telephone is assembled on a black lower part, containing all functional units. Customer variants in the form of colour and text take place when the upper part is assembled.

This family of toy animals from Lego is assembled on the same assembly equipment. The body parts are uniform but vary according to colour. The heads are fixed manually in the assembly fixture while the rest of the assembly is fully automatic.

6.5 Achieving a GOOD WORKING ENVIRONMENT

There is naturally a lot of variation between the designer's ideals and the working environment within an assembly system; one can still, however, indicate connections and principles. It must be emphasised again that the principles cannot be applied correctly to all areas, and there may indeed be some areas where they are completely inappropriate.

| | Automation can cause improvement in the environment 6.13 |

This principle is manifest when one considers freeing the operator from dangerous, uncomfortable or tiring jobs.

In many cases the introduction of assembly equipment will mean an improvement in the working environment, e.g. in the form of noise reduction, operator relief and increased job motivation.

This Nordson robot is used in spraying and ensures a uniform quality of surface treatment. Simultaneously the possibility of personnel coming into contact with poisonous fumes is avoided.

Working conditions in a telephone factory today and 30 years ago. The division of production and assembly in conjunction with the phasing out of machining have lead to the establishment of a beneficial working environment. (GNT Automatic).

Avoid "dangerous" assembly principles   (Principle 6.14)

Those running production cannot completely eliminate uncomfortable, dangerous or poisonous elements in an assembly process – the designer however, can. He can take advantage of the degrees of freedom at his disposal to find different structures and thereby alter assembly processes.

Handling equipment from C & J Machines Ltd. By using such equipment in conjunction with pressure die casting equipment one can achieve better productivity and better product quality – as a result of a uniform machine cycle. In addition, the operator is relieved of the need to perform the monotonous job of unloading the machines.

Welding of steel construction with the aid of a Motoman L10 welding robot. The human welder/ supervisor is no longer exposed to the welding fumes.

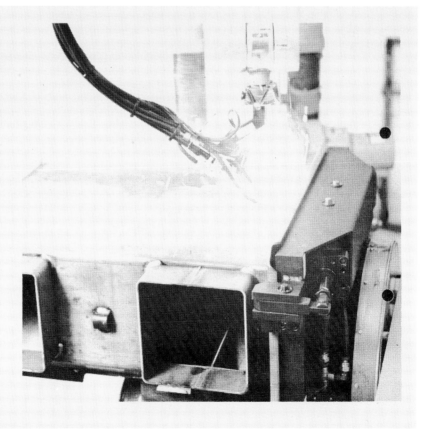

6.6 Review

Chapter 6 has dealt with the following principles and postulations for assembly oriented determination of goal setting in assembly and product assortment.

ASSEMBLY GOALS and PRODUCT ASSORTMENT

Principles:

6.1 Assembly requires quality control

6.2 Automatic assembly requires a considerable quality increase

6.3 Assembly is (also) a management problem

6.4 Design for mechanized assembly

6.5 Design for automatic assembly

6.6 Design for flexible automatic assembly

6.7 Manual assembly has many virtues!

6.8 Eliminate assembly

6.9 Design for standard equipment

6.10 Design for special equipment

6.11 Avoid variants

6.12 Make the variants uniform in assembly

6.13 Automation may cause improvement in environment

6.14 Avoid "dangerous" assembly principles

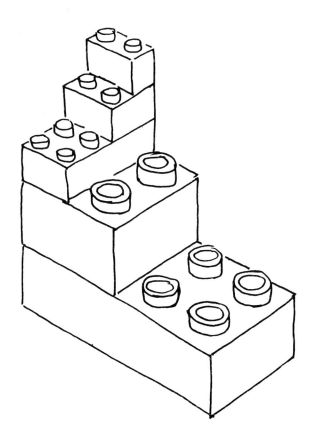

Design for ease of assembly

– systemize the product's structure

SUMMARY

The designer determines the product's structure and the component's design. It is important to remember the degrees of design freedom at every stage of the design phase, degrees which create the possibility for an optimisation of assembly.

Assuming the general principle, that design should be simple and clear, we will deal with a series of principles and guide lines concerning choice of product structure (section 7.4) and choice of joining method (section 7.5).

7.1 Is assembly necessary?

In chapter 2 we explained the reasons for assembly, that is to say the design deliberations and technical necessities which lead to assembly.

The principle construction of the product decides which individual parts it will consist of; normally however one chooses a much finer division of machine parts based on a series of varying requirements or necessities. Fig. 7.1 illustrates a paper punch, firstly in principle, secondly as a functional structuring and finally in the phase of production and assembly-oriented structuring.

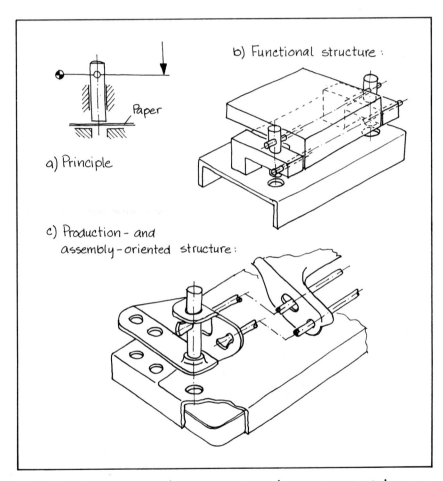

Fig. 7.1. A paper punch construction shown in principle, as a functional structure and in the production and assembly-oriented structure.

What is the designer's taste?

If we wish to design for ease of assembly we must understand how the designer determines the product's structure and how he determines the design of the machine parts as shown in Fig. 7.1.

The starting point is, in the case of a new design at any rate, a group of idealistic solutions which can realise the various functions in the product, i.e. hinging, sliding, hole punching, power amplification, returning etc., in Figure 7.1.

The designer will now attempt to apply these functions in a space frame, i.e. to work out an ideal structure where these functions can be combined in an advantageous way. The first step in this structuring is to allow the individual material interfaces to be defined so that the product can be divided into machine parts.

The next natural step is to quantify the structure, i.e. to decide on distance, angles, tolerances, diameters, etc., and to determine the structure's division of form, i.e. its division into machine parts. Then each individual part's function is defined, as well as its functional surface and relation to the other machine parts.

The products parts are thereby defined and detail design can commence. Here form, material dimensions, tolerance and surface quality are determined for each machine part, so that the unit takes shape as planned.

Design degrees of freedom

Several steps in this area of design activity contain many degrees of freedom, i.e. the possibility to create alternative solutions and thereby adapt the product to the demands and strive for an optimal product, see Fig. 7.2.

Design for ease of assembly can be achieved by observing these design degrees of freedom through assembly "spectacles" –and using the opportunities presented.

Assembly spectacles

One can attempt to apply various assembly principles at every stage. As we mentioned earlier, a good result can often be achieved, but particular conditions can apply which render the principle inapplicable.

How to avoid assembly/facilitate assembly

Fig. 7.2 illustrates that one can concentrate on structuring as well as choice of process (hereby including naturally material and form choices). These two "points of attack" form the subject of the next section; firstly, however, we will turn our attention to some general factors which affect the task of structuring.

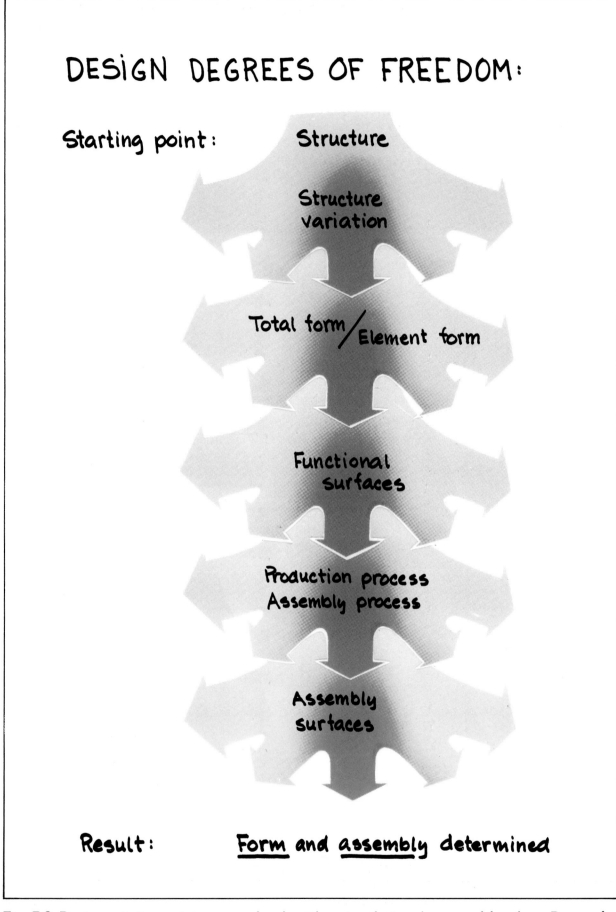

Fig. 7.2. Design activity contains many levels with many design degrees of freedom. Design for ease of assembly represents exploitation of the ideal solutions from the assembly standpoint.

7.2 Some important product factors

The design of a product is subject to a long series of considerations of factors, which can be classified as shown in Fig. 7.3.

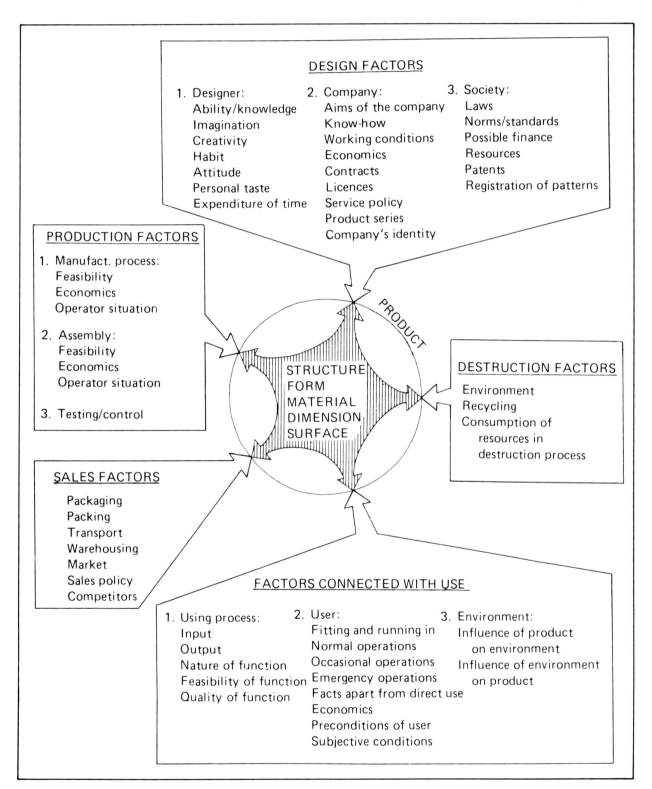

Fig. 7.3. Survey of product factors in order of phases in the product's life. Particularly note the production factors, including assembly which create demands on the product's basic characteristics, shown in the middle (4).

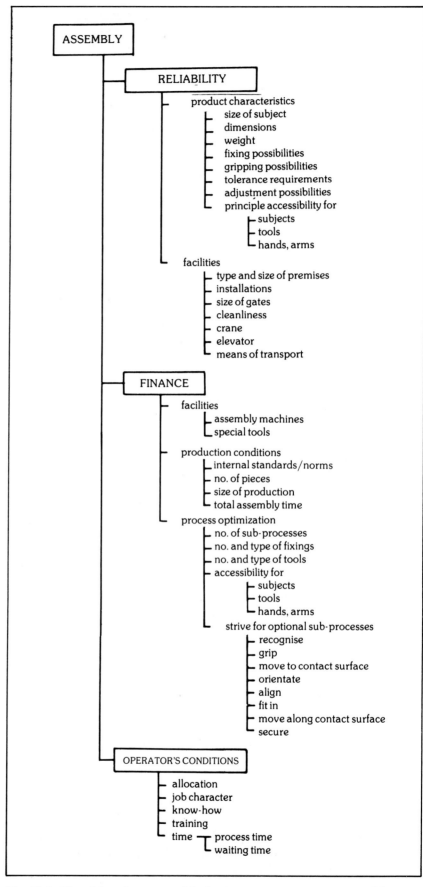

Fig. 7.4. Checklist for assembly factors, containing general factors relevant for the designer who can exercise influence over the structuring of the product (12). This publication extends the area to cover more general factors.

When we discuss design for ease of assembly, we focus naturally on certain of the production-technical factors, primarily assembly; we do this by regarding production as a whole (i.e. considering all production factors), as only in this way can we achieve an optimal result.

Some salient questions are grouped in Fig. 7.4 as a type of checklist of the most important production factors; these emphasise that the standpoint in this chapter is the product's structuring.

7.3 Two general principles

Two principles apply to the structuring of a product, which most often lead to improvements in quality (in every respect), and assembly, namely those of "simplicity" and "clarity". These principles do not require any further introduction as they are clarified by the examples given.

| Design simply. | (Principle 7.1) |

– so that one can speak totally of an optimal solution – few parts, few and simple assemblies.

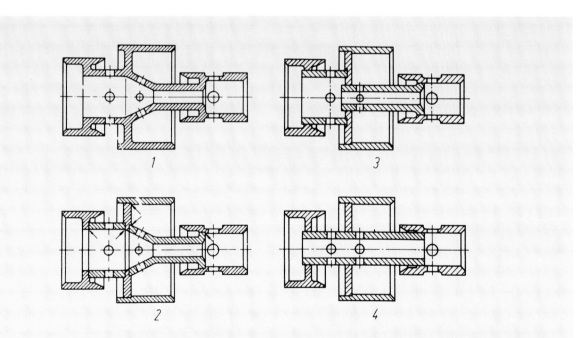

Simplification of a 100mm long valve. 1: Casting is difficult and expensive. 2: Better solution with simple parts which can be assembled by hard soldering. 3: Simplification of the central tube-shaped part. 4: Additional possibilities for simplification, assuming that comparable axial surfaces are not required. (13).

Note that the starting point is a complex item that does not require assembly, whilst the optimal solution contains several simple components.

– so that the production and assembly processes can be clearly executed.
– so that the product will not be statically indeterminate.
– so that eventual adjustments do not work against each other.

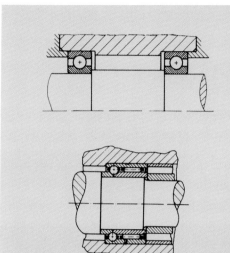

a. The bearing's functional ability depends on the pre-loading, and this cannot be guaranteed because of thermal expansion. Assembly can be problematic if the components are not manufactured to specific tolerances.

b. Combined roller/thrust bearing where the radial forces transmission is imprecise (13).

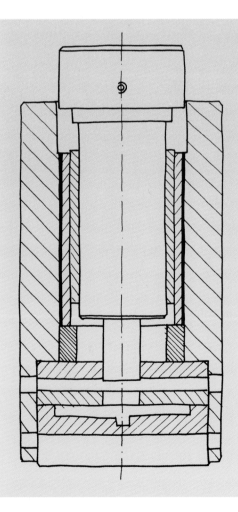

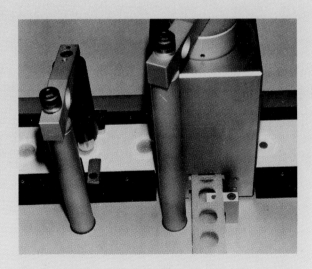

Punching tool with a very simple construction. Drawing at left shows how the cylindrical sleeve is aligned with the punching tool by means of a cast liner (heavy black lines). Illustration above shows the punching tool fixed on an assembly machine. Section 9.4 deals with this example in detail.

7.4 Choice of product structure

Product structuring can be tackled in many ways, namely:

– by means of the current construction principle:

★ integrate
★ differentiate.
★ use of total chassis
★ design a stacked product
★ apply compound-construction
★ design sound base components
★ construct product of building blocks.
★ see principles in Chapter 6
★ construct product as in a building box system
★ construct product by use of correct standards.
★ avoid high tolerance demands on the elements
★ avoid high surface demands on the elements.

It can be difficult to envisage the application of these in an existing product and correspondingly difficult to grasp the fact that other modes of structuring do exist – in other words, design degrees of freedom.

The next section wdeal with the principles in detail. We hope that these examples can act both as explanation and inspiration, even though they are possibly inapplicable to the task the particular reader is confronted with.

| Integrate. | (Principle 7.3) |

in order to achieve:

– few components and sub-assemblies
– larger and thereby easier handled subjects
– full exploitation of the capability of the production process.

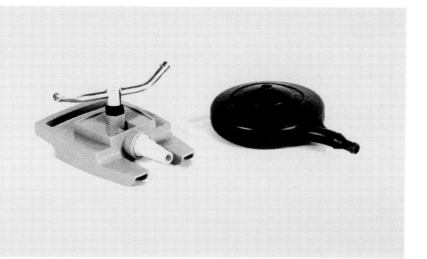

Water sprinkler in two different models. The function is the same but the difference in the construction (and thereby number of components) is great.

103

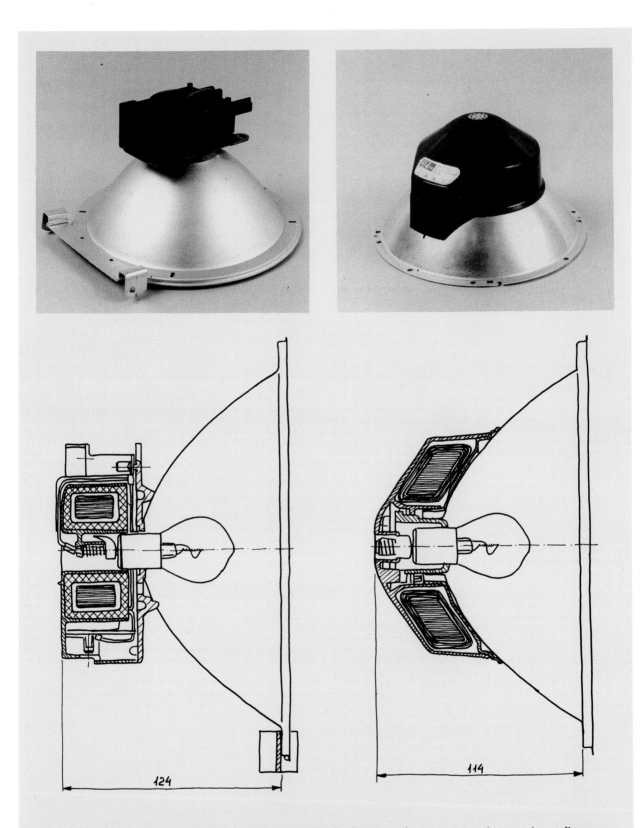

Unitraf is a compact composed unit, comprised of a transformer, a socket and a reflector. The old model is shown at left and the newer, Unitraf, on the right. The new product is *integrated* in many respects: Structurally, in that the transformer's exterior is the housing and bears the reflector. Form-wise in that the transformer is circular in order to save space (the rolled collar is simply pressed out into the form shown). Electrically, in that the transformer's terminals are soldered directly to the lamp socket and spade lugs. See also example on page 124. (Danish Signal Industry)

Bearing housing (a) is produced as a compound construction (casting and welding). This could be replaced by a completely cast housing, thus eliminating assembly. 36% of the production cost can be saved by adopting this design alteration (13).

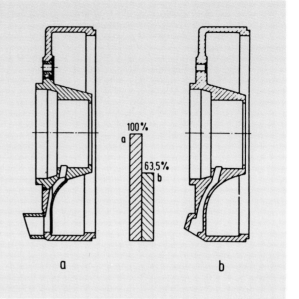

in order to achieve:

– differentiated adaptability to functional demands

– process-wise adaptability to the firm's production apparatus (standard machine tools)

– possibility to apply bought parts and standardised parts

– fewer and lighter subjects

– increase in size of annual production.

Differing degrees of material differentiation. The optimal solution depends on number of pieces, working life requirements, component and production price, including assembly costs.

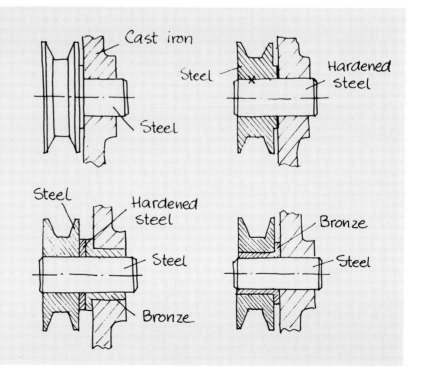

105

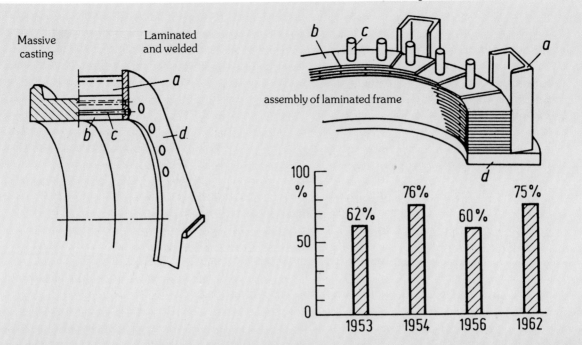

Massive casting

Laminated and welded

assembly of laminated frame

A magnet frame for a big DC dynamo can be produced either as a massive cast part or as a laminated and welded block. In the lattter case the process is a casting of the steel block, milling, punching, assembly, compression and riveting up of the laminated block and finally welding of the housing. The production costs have for many years remained at a lower level for the laminated solution, though this is dependent to some extent on the market. See also photo on page 46 (13).

| Use a total chassis: | (Principle 7.5) |

in order to:
- avoid adjustments

- achieve a good basis for the assembly operations, including transport, checking, testing, etc.

Two generations of chassis for a strip perforator from GNT Automatic. The older on the left is cast and screwed, the chassis on the right is of punched and bent plates.

106

The picture on the left shows a chassis for a photo-copying machine from Rex-Rotary, built from punched and bent steel plates, welded together into a highly precise component. All functional parts are mounted on this chassis by conveyor belt assembly without adjustments. Great emphasis was placed on the concept of design simplicity for assembly (see principle 7.2).

Design a stacked product	(Principle 7.6)

in order to achieve:
– simple assemblies.

By "stacked product" one means a product structure where most of the components are laid in "stacks" and are finally secured by the internal cohesion of the stack components.

This classic and simple example shows the principle of a stacked product. The two parts of the plug contain (when joined), all components in the plug (at left). By comparison the plug on the right was not constructed as a stacked product.

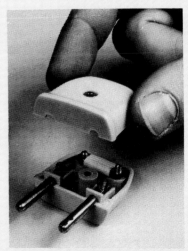

107

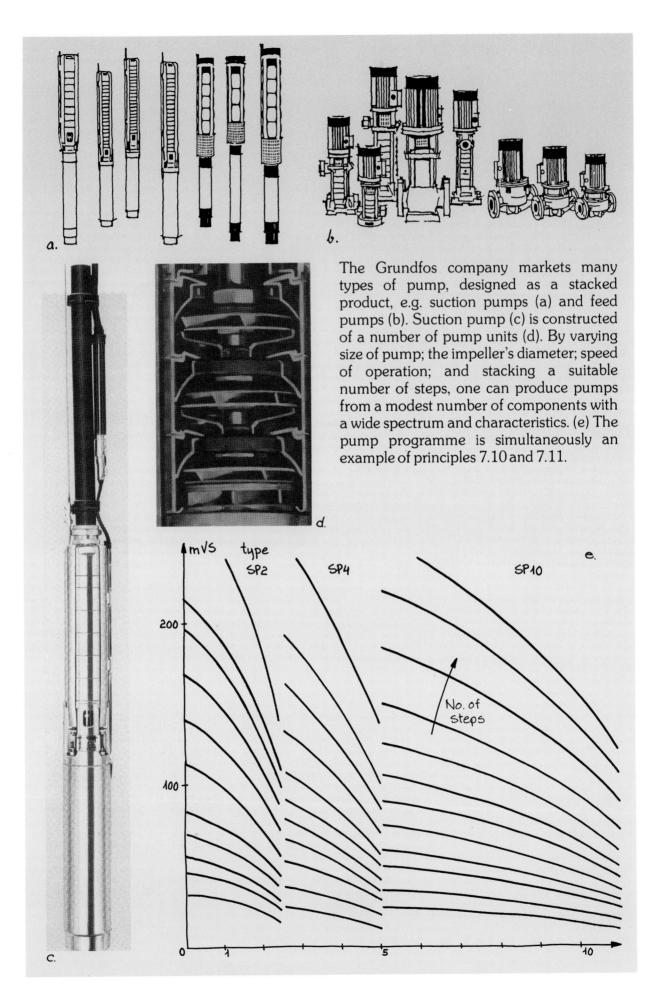

a.

b.

The Grundfos company markets many types of pump, designed as a stacked product, e.g. suction pumps (a) and feed pumps (b). Suction pump (c) is constructed of a number of pump units (d). By varying size of pump; the impeller's diameter; speed of operation; and stacking a suitable number of steps, one can produce pumps from a modest number of components with a wide spectrum and characteristics. (e) The pump programme is simultaneously an example of principles 7.10 and 7.11.

c.

d.

e.

mVS

type
SP2   SP4   SP10

No. of
steps

200

100

0   1   5   10

in order to achieve:

– optimal exploitation of various materials

– a complex structure by means of basic processes

– clear, process-determined assembly.

By compound construction we mean a structure of machine parts made of various materials which are joined to a permanent structure.

This rotor for a hydro-electric generator is compound constructed by means of welding together of three materials: (a) of G.S. 45.1 arms, (b) of Mst. 52-3 and rotor ring (c) of G.S. 45-9.

This design replaces constructions joined by bolts or welded in uniformly expensive material. The alternative allows optimal used materials for the individual tasks.

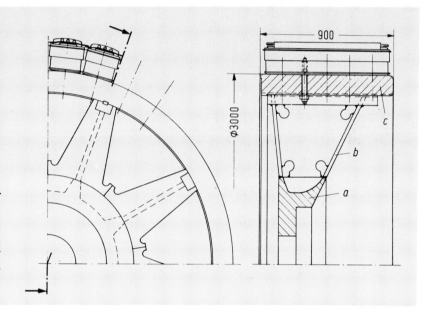

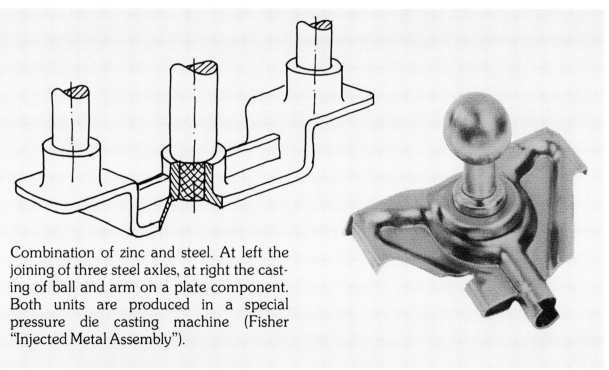

Combination of zinc and steel. At left the joining of three steel axles, at right the casting of ball and arm on a plate component. Both units are produced in a special pressure die casting machine (Fisher "Injected Metal Assembly").

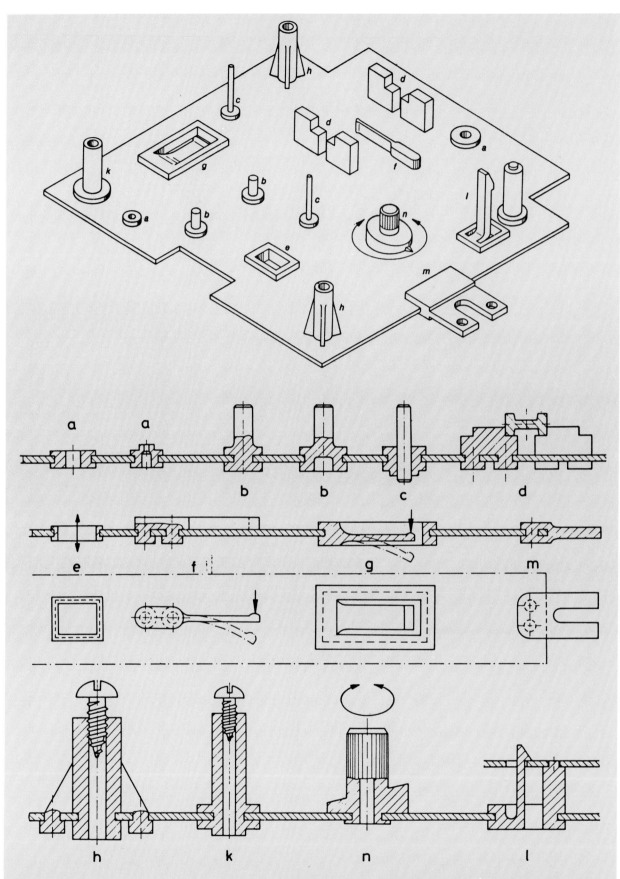

Examples of some of the possibilities of the in situ moulding technique (Hoechst). All details are injection moulded in/onto a metal plate, which has been inserted into the mould.

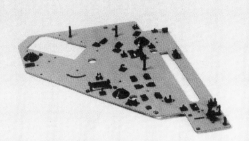

Application of in situ moulding technique in a chassis for a Bang & Olufsen gramophone. This chassis replaces a model with steel chassis and components assembled onto it. By using this technique one can achieve considerable reductions in assembly time and – by reason of the processes's high degree of accuracy – reduction of adjustment time.

In addition to the example of compound construction mentioned previously one can refer to plastic covered steel plates which are punched and pressed to form a chassis or a similar construction, compound-constructed, sound proofing panels, lightweight panels composed of hexagonal cells of thin aluminium stuck to steel plates for planes.

| | Design good basis components | (Principle 7.8) |

in order to:

– achieve a good basis for transport, fixing and force effects in joining processes.

– avoid assembly fixtures.

The design principles of basic components are dealt with in section 8.3, see also examples beneath and on p. 142.

Tape recorder chassis from Hitachi. The chassis is designed so as to form a basis for later assemblies; it can be transported from assembly automat to assembly automat without extra fixtures.

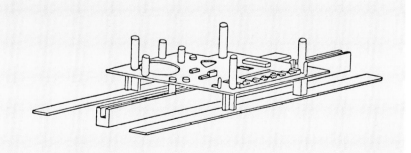

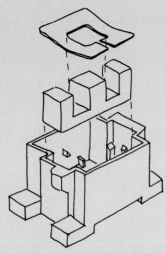

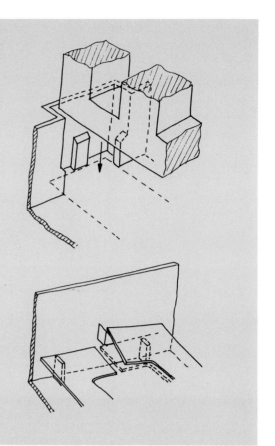

In this contactor the housing's lower part acts as the base component for the manned assembly. Note the guide fins and the locking plate's fastening. (Danfoss Ltd.) At right is shown how the surfaces on the housing's interior guide the core in place and how the locking plate glides into place over a triangular lug – without being able to move the opposite way.

Construct the product of building blocks   (Principle 7.9)

in order to:

– be able to apply parallel assembly.

– achieve flexible assembly planning.

– achieve advantages in that one can test or eventually replace larger units in the product.

By the term "building block" we mean a larger, independent structured part of a product, which is a functional unit with simple relations to the rest of the product.

Bearings are a simple example of building blocks. (NTN-bearings).

Television from Bang & Olufsen constructed of building blocks of both structural and functional character.

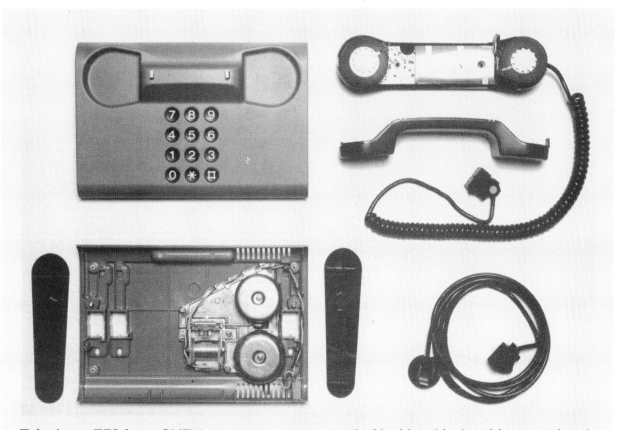

Telephone F78 from GNT Automatic is constructed of building blocks of functional and structural character. The telephone's electronic part is placed on the rear of the upper part and carries the buttons.

so that:

– the series size for the sub-systems is increased.

– parallel production, assembly and testing become possible.

– the product's assembly is made simpler, less complicated.

By "building box system" one means a system of products which are structured in such a way that all products can be constructed of a number of building stones.

The building box, i.e. the composition of building stones can be determined in various ways, as shown in Fig. 7.5. The goal of such a principle is to achieve a product variant programme with a minimum of variant costs. As discussed in chapter 5 the product as a whole can be structured to be sympathetic to assembly or this can apply to the product's sub-systems. The figure shows some principally different modes of structuring building boxes.

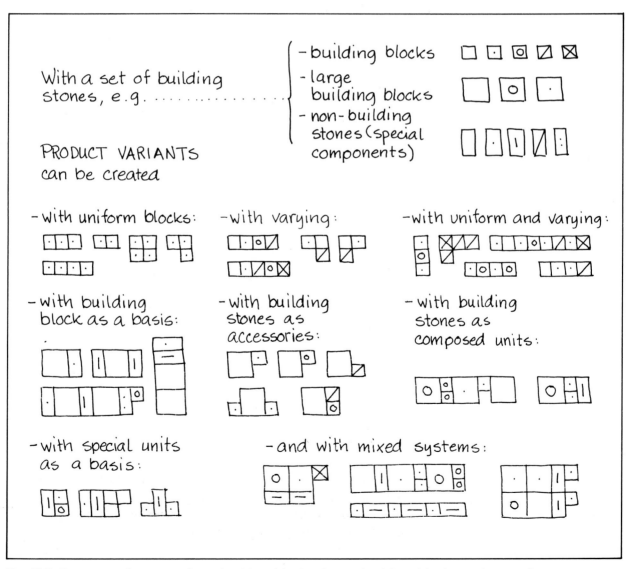

Fig. 7.5. Creation of variants from building blocks, larger building blocks and special components.

Occasionally the building box principle is combined with other structuring principles, for example so that the product variants make up a series of standard units or a module system (see structure principle 7.11 and examples below).

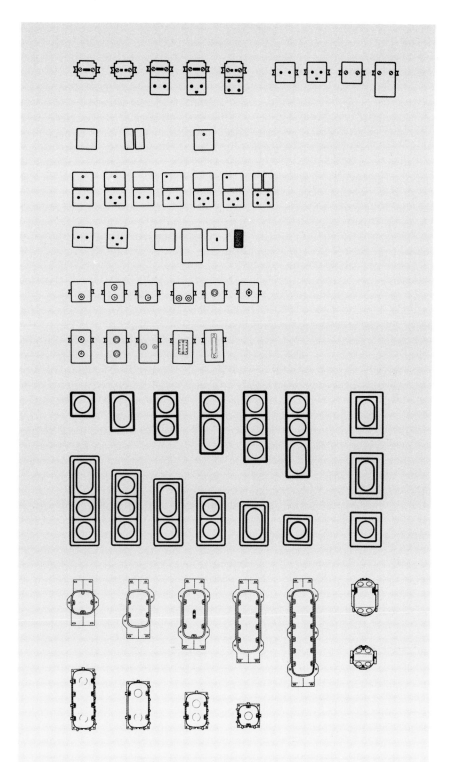

Building box system from LK-NES including cage (switches and plugs in various forms), covering, signal switch, frames in various widths as well as sockets for bricking-in or building-in. This assortment can provide the answer to most installation tasks.

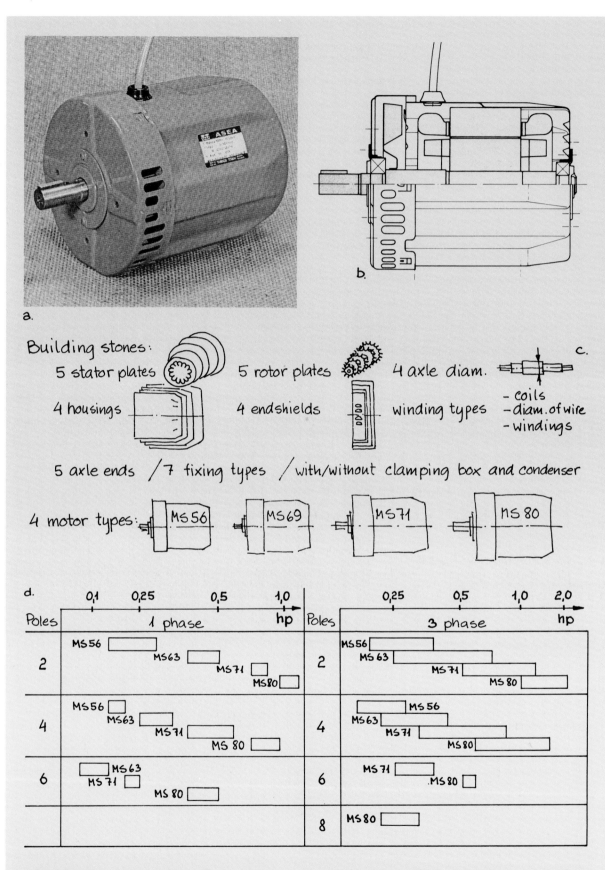

A building box system from Titan/Asea composed five sizes of stators and rotors, of four types of motors which can cover a large power range (d). Building stones (c) are in four shaft diameters and additionally the windings can be varied. An enormous motor programme can be derived from the motor variations and accessories.

so that:

– series size for the components is increased.

– standard, bought and re-usable parts are exploited.

National and international standards have, among others, the goal of increasing the use of particular goods, i.e. raw materials, part-assemblies, components and sub-systems. Use of standard parts in a product can range from a banal use of standard screws to use of standardised control units, regulators, motors, lens combinations etc.

Internal company standards can in the same way increase the use of frequently-appearing units and thereby dramatically increase series size and correspondingly decrease assembly costs, by means of using known assemblies and eventually known equipment for assembly.

This photomontage shows the results of assortment rational-isation carried out at De Smithske A/S. The pump programme now comprises a series of standard units, i.e. the pump's performance range is so distributed that a small number of types can cover prevailing customer require-ments. This limitation of assortment and particularly limitation of variants has, naturally, a favourable influence on assembly.

so that:

– production costs are reduced.

Precise placement of elements or functional surfaces in relation to each other can be achieved by manufacturing and assembling parts with precise tolerances, by adjusting into place or by using fixtures or gauges.

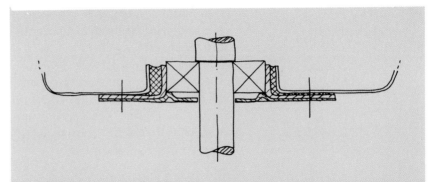

This example illustrates how one can avoid high demands of tolerance on bearing caps for example for electric motors, by using epoxy-moulding material.

so that:

– production costs are reduced.

– handling during assembly can ignore vulnerability.

This Grundfos pump is painted just before assembly is completed. After painting the electric box and type plate are assembled.

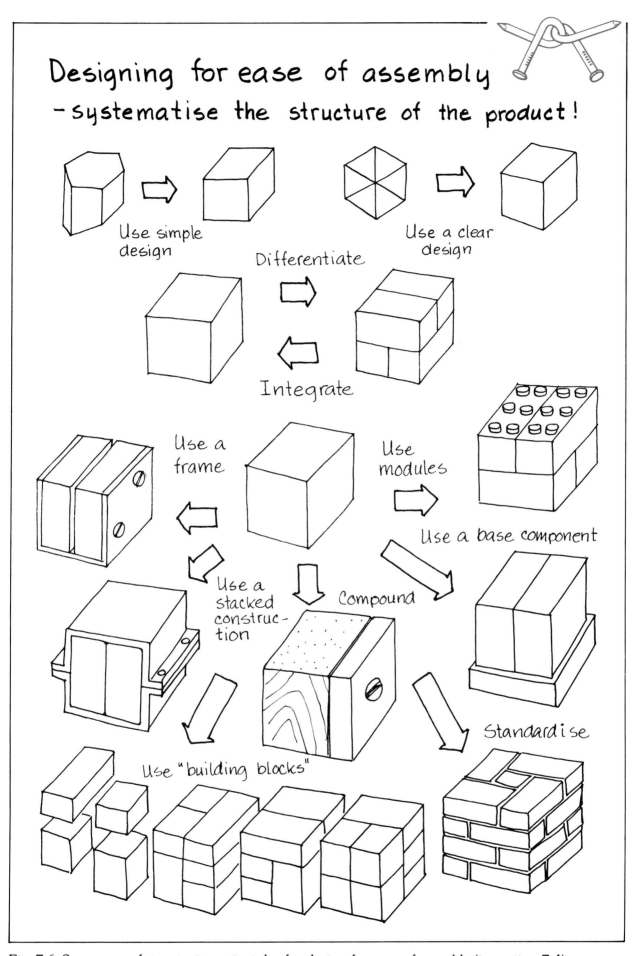

Fig. 7.6. Summary of structuring principles for design for ease of asembly (in section 7.4).

7.5 Choice of joining method

The assembly costs and the resulting quality depend decisively on the method of joining and the way it is carried out. The joining methods which are available to the designer make up, as shown in section 2.1, a large, motley troop. Which one should one select?

Naturally there are masses of guide-lines and a wealth of experience in the area of certain types of product, material combinations and trades. Whilst it does not lie within the scope of this book to deal with the problem of how a particular assembly operation is designed and achieved – certain general principles are mentioned.

| | Avoid assemblies | (Principle 7.14) |

– and thereby reduce such costs to zero.

This radical principle is manifest, but often demands a new train of thought or a breaking of new ground in order to be applied. Some check questions can possibly lead to a solution:

★ Can differing material characteristics be combined?

The part of the gear illustrated is composed of three elements which make up gear and bearing. Polyacetal can be used instead of steel and brass, whereby the three elements are integrated into one and assembly is avoided.

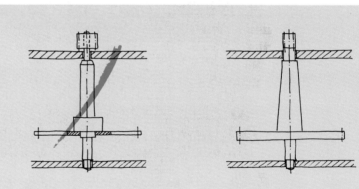

Pressure die cast gear in Hostaform C27021. In this design one has achieved a reduction of inertial forces at start and stop, and simultaneously achieved a non-backlash transfer without having to apply tough tolerance demands.

★ Can flexibility be achieved through elasticity?

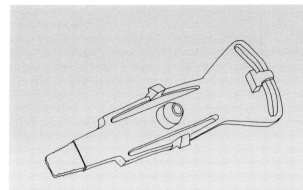

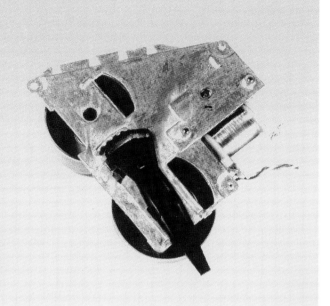

Volume control in GNT Automatics telephone. The plastic arm exploits the following material characteristics – stiffness in the form of power transmission, integral cam locking of the arm, bearing characteristics, elasticity in the outer arc for indexation.

Hose clamp made of metal (six components) and plastic (one component). Assembly is eliminated by taking advantage of the elasticity of the non-metallic components.

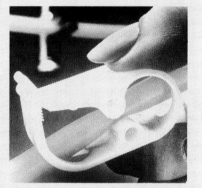

★ Do the parts have to be able to be de-assembled?

A cap and screws can be replaced with a tin or plastic disc, which is pressed into place or fixed in a slot.

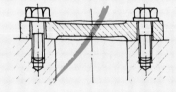

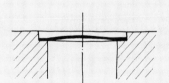

Re-design of a screwed plug, previously made of metal. New model: plastic to be pressed in (10).

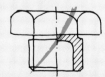

121

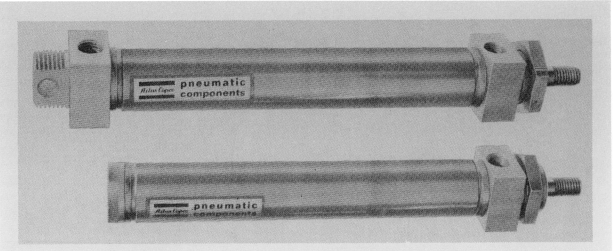

The cylinder pipe in these pneumatic cylinders from ATLAS COPCO is rolled over the end caps and can therefore not be disassembled without destruction.

An opening that is normally covered by a plate fixed by screws can be covered by means of a punched and bent plate which is fitted with the aid of a simple tool.

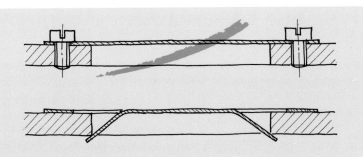

Avoid separate composing elements   (Principle 7.15)

— so that one avoids handling of (small) components.

See examples below and on the following pages.

The joining of a plate housing was previously achieved by means of special screw compositions. Integral key bars can be used instead (10).

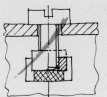
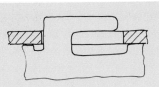

A headed pin is used to secure the angular plate. The illustration at right shows how the lock can be formed as an integral part of the component.

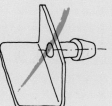

122

Signal switch from LK-NES contains two examples of assembly without separate joining elements. Left: the contact spring's fixing by means of ultrasonic welding of the plastic material housing, right, how the wire is fixed under the contact spring without using composing elements or special tools.

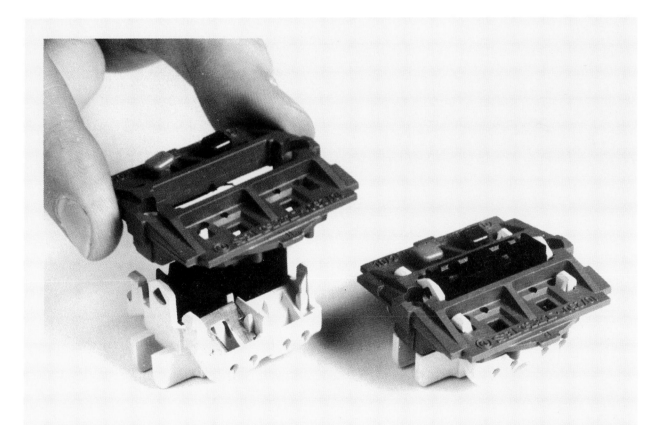

This mains switch from LK-NES is assembled either manually or automatically. The switch is designed to be assembled by stacking. When the components are in place, the base and cover are assembled as shown. Four sets of hooks go through the cover and hold the switch together.

These terminals are fixed in the spool with the aid of barbs. The terminals are almost pushed into place, the wires from the spools are soldered on, whereafter the terminals are pressed home. The spool's wire connections are hereby relieved. (Danfoss Ltd.)

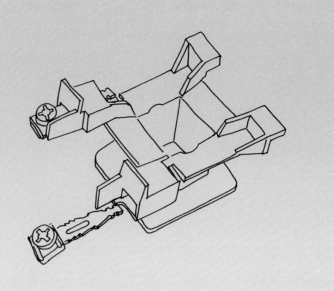

Steel covering plate assembled with screws and nuts can be replaced by an injection moulded plastic plate with simple locking buttons.

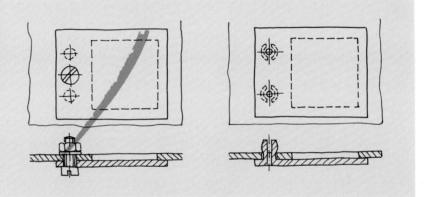

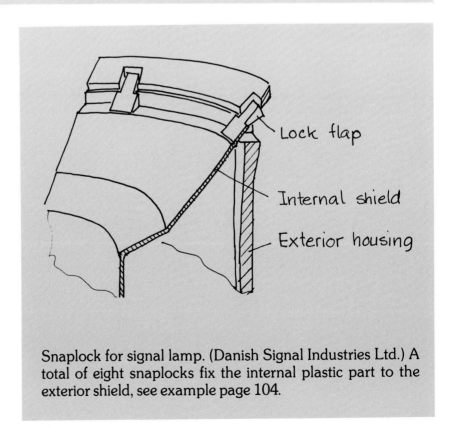

Lock flap

Internal shield

Exterior housing

Snaplock for signal lamp. (Danish Signal Industries Ltd.) A total of eight snaplocks fix the internal plastic part to the exterior shield, see example page 104.

– where the tools or method of production create forms which replace components or promote joining in the actual process.

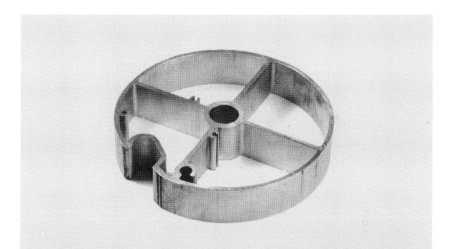

The roller which bears the master in a Rex-Rotary 5080 copying machine is designed as a large extruded aluminium profile as shown in the illustrated cross-section. A number of assembly operations are avoided by means of this integrating method of production.

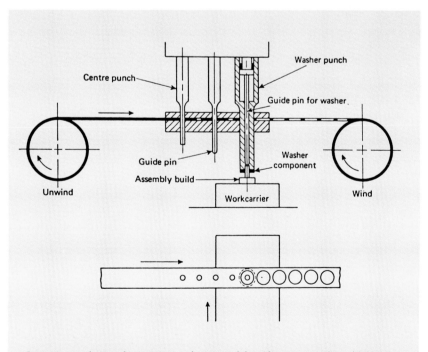

Integrated production and assembly of tension disc (11).

125

This corner element in a building system (electric panels) is composed of bent and pressed plates. Every connection is fixed by means of two countersunk screws. (LØGSTRUP)

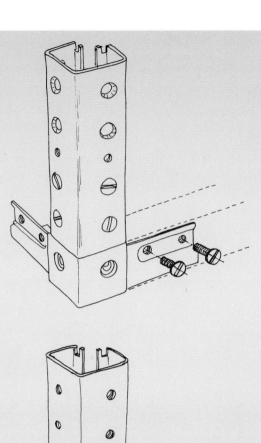

An improved model is here designed as a cast block (zinc), with tapped holes. A deep depression is formed in each connecting bar so that socket head cap screws can be fitted in line with the imposed forces, i.e. only tension forces are applied to the screws. (LØGSTRUP)

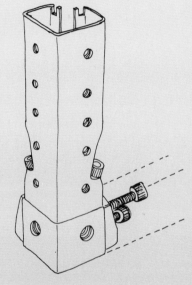

In this version the corner is once again as a cast component, but with longer control surfaces. The connecting bars are fixed by a set screw which is fitted in the corner block and applies pressure on a small protruding indentation in every connecting rod. (CUBIC)

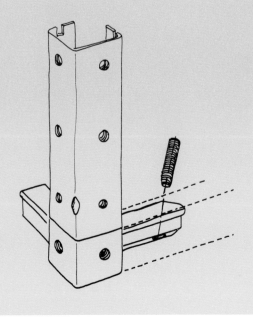

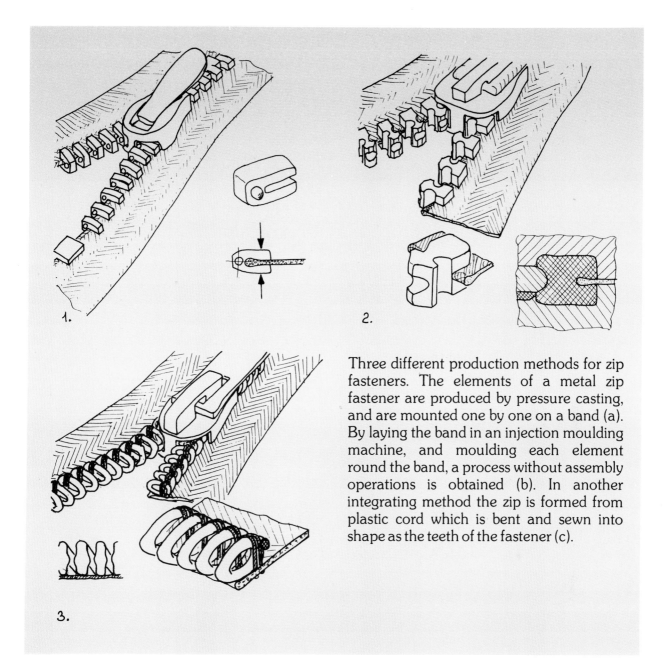

Three different production methods for zip fasteners. The elements of a metal zip fastener are produced by pressure casting, and are mounted one by one on a band (a). By laying the band in an injection moulding machine, and moulding each element round the band, a process without assembly operations is obtained (b). In another integrating method the zip is formed from plastic cord which is bent and sewn into shape as the teeth of the fastener (c).

7.6 Review

PRODUCT STRUCTURING FOR
DESIGN FOR EASE OF ASSEMBLY

Principles:

<u>General</u>:

7.1   – design simply

7.2   – design clearly

<u>Choose the correct structural principle</u>:

7.3   – integrate

7.4   – diffentiate

7.5   – use a total chassis

7.6   – design a stacked product

7.7   – use compound design

7.8   – design good basis components

7.9   – design a product of building blocks

7.10 – design the product as a building box system

7.11 – design the product using norms

7.12 – avoid tolerance demands on components

7.13 – avoid surface demands on components

<u>Choose the correct joining method</u>:

7.14 – avoid assemblies

7.15 – avoid separate composing elements

7.16 – use integrating production methods

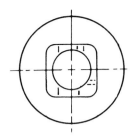

Design for ease of assembly
– design the components so as to be suited to assembly

SUMMARY

The product's structure determines the components' design and the assembly problems; all the same, care must be exercised in the components' design for ease of assembly. Deliberations as to the assembly surfaces can act as a fruitful basis for such determinations.

Design for ease of automatic assembly normally means that the product can also be easily assembled manually.

A series of principles, taking account of various assembly operations, will be dealt with and examined. Section 8.4 provides an overall review of these.

8.1 The connection between product structure and component design

There is only a limited rationalisation effect to be gained when one evaluates only a product's components with a view to easier assembly. A much greater effect can be achieved by tackling the product's structure or considering the product assortment more thoroughly in conjunction with the setting of goals for a rationalisation of assembly.

On the other hand, rationalisation will have no effect if the components are not satisfactory assembly-wise, in other words, the assembly intentions are taken right up to the stage of well-designed components. The product's structure determines, as explained in Chapter 7, the component's design in relation to assembly and therefore directly the assembly problems which arise.

Design for ease of assembly will in practice be executed as a reciprocal action between structural deliberation and deliberations concerning design form. Figure 8.1 shows the result of a

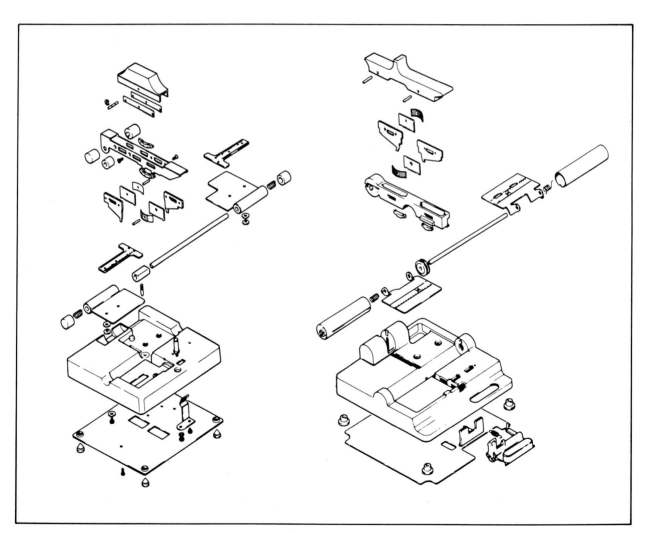

Fig. 8.1. Film press in two versions, old and new. In the newer model the number of parts has been reduced from 79 to 29. An important rationalisation assembly-wise was achieved by means of an evaluation study. (AGFA). See text.

design task on a film press. By comparing the two illustrations it can be seen that changes have been made in the mechanical principles (locking system), in the product structure (the number of components has been reduced by means of numerous integrations, e.g. the two scales are now integrated on the two hinged plates, the bearing frame is integrated into the chassis), in the production process used, in the type of components (bearings, springs, ferrule), and in the detailed design (snaplock, integrated fasteners).

The components' determining characteristics

It is useful to realise that a component is completely determined by specifying:

> Form, material, dimensions, surface quality and tolerances.

Assembly-oriented solutions will be dependent on the correct specification of these characteristics. Many of them will be of importance, but the form is decisive in so far as certain surfaces have the task of realising the assembly.

Assembly surfaces

Those surfaces which define a component (make up the component's form) have various tasks. The component has one or more functions (support, transfer forces, lead etc.) which are realised by the *functional surfaces* (see Fig. 8.2). Among these are the surfaces which constitute the relationship with other components, i.e. those which touch or lie next to other components. These surfaces are called *connecting surfaces* (in Fig. 8.2 these are identical to the functional surfaces). The surfaces which are not functional surfaces are termed *free surfaces*.

By "assembly surfaces" is meant those surfaces which are used in the handling stage of the assembly process, e.g. for arranging, transport, positioning, as leading surfaces etc., but which have no function from the product's point of view, when assembly is completed.

One can use either functional surfaces or free surfaces as assembly surfaces. Functional surfaces cannot normally be altered in favour of assembly, but free surfaces can. A profitable technique at the assembly deliberation stage is to mark in colour the descriptions and relationship of functional, assembly and free surfaces for each component.

A given component can, schematically expressed, be suited to assembly by:

- exploiting given functional surfaces and free surfaces for assembly.

- removing materials/changing the form of the free surfaces.

- adding materials/changing the form of the free surfaces.

131

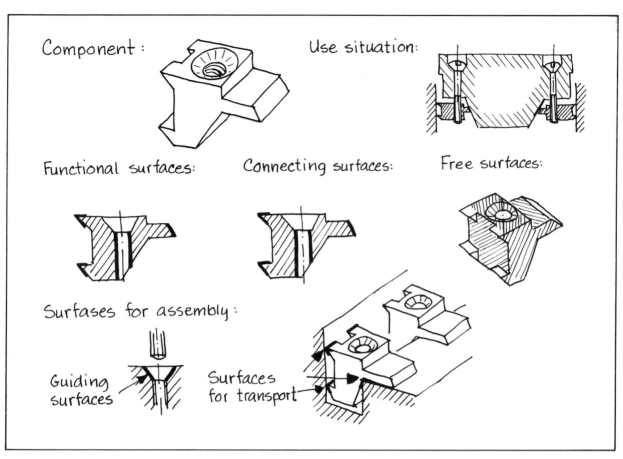

Fig. 8.2. Clamping piece from an LK-NES switch. The function of this component is to keep the switch in the fitting box. Functional surfaces, connecting surfaces, free surfaces and surfaces for assembly are shown.

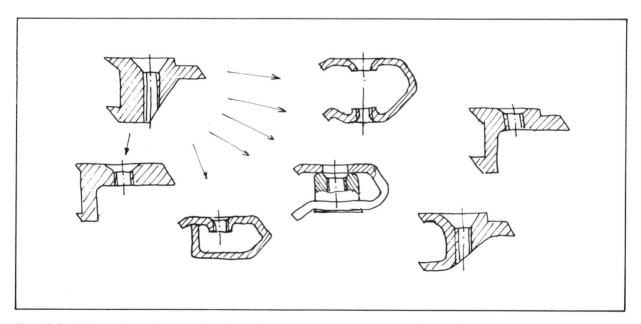

Fig. 8.3. Alternative designs for the clamping piece shown in Fig. 8.2. Analysis may show that these are easy to assemble.

These manipulations are naturally closely connected to the product process deliberations and, as a result, the total financial picture of the product. An example with starting point in Fig. 8.2 is shown in Fig. 8.3.

8.2 Manual or automatic assembly?

The examples used in this book focus on those subjects and areas where mechanical and/or automatic assembly can represent a relevant alternative to manual assembly. We will therefore exclude the principles which are applied to traditional manual assembly, e.g. in automobile, ship and agricultural machinery branches.

What relationship is there between design for ease of assembly for manual assembly and versus that of mechanical/automatic assembly?

One can generally assume:

> PRODUCTS FOR AUTOMATIC ASSEMBLY ARE EASY TO ASSEMBLY MANUALLY.

Though this does not apply to certain operations demanding special degrees of power or accuracy. A good guideline for ease of automatic assembly is therefore:

> DESIGN THE PRODUCT SO THAT IT IS EASY TO ASSEMBLE MANUALLY – CONSEQUENTLY IT IS HIGHLY PROBABLE THAT IT WILL BE EASILY ASSEMBLED AUTOMATICALLY.

The following section will deal with certain common principles of component design for ease of assembly, primarily related to automatic assembly.

8.3 Considering assembly operations

The operations of the assembly process were dealt with in Chapter 3, see summary on pages 31-33. Design for ease of assembly of components demands that consideration is paid to these operations, but it would be exaggerating to state principles for every single operation. In practice it has been observed that one should primarily consider the following operations:

ORIENTATE
TRANSPORT
MERGING
JOINING

The joining operation was dealt with in section 7.5. In the following section the principles and examples related to these operations will be examined. This examination will be introduced by means of some general principles, whereby several of the stated assembly operations can be avoided. It should, however, be borne in mind that principles must not be regarded as absolute but as guidelines that should normally be followed but can, in certain situations, be inapplicable.

so that:

- difficult handling is avoided

- critical positioning or inlaying is avoided

- the total number of operations is reduced.

The push buttons for GNT Automatic's telephones are injection moulded in two steps in an injection mould, so that the white figure remains fixed to the black background. The buttons are fixed in a frame which comprises a part of the product until the buttons are mounted into the contact system.

The terminals in this Bang & Olufsen pick-up are mounted as a unit. When they are attached the connecting piece is cut away.

This principle is dealt with in section 7.5.

Use magazines   (Principle 8.2)

"Magazining" means a mechanical form or frame which partially or wholly maintains the components in a constant orientation.

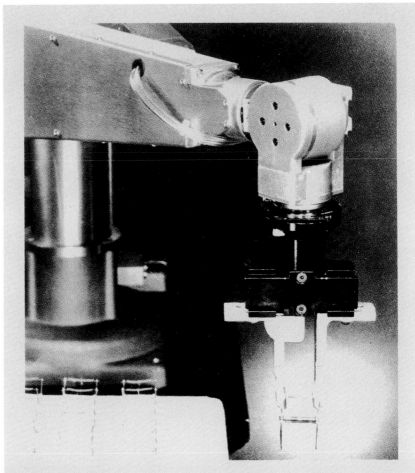

Magazine for filaments. The components transported in these magazines between the various production processes.

The use of the word "bandform" must not be taken literally here. It embraces simple punched components which hang together before assembly, bent or pre-assembled sub-assemblies which are connected, or components which, with the help of bearing material (band, foil, etc.) are connected.

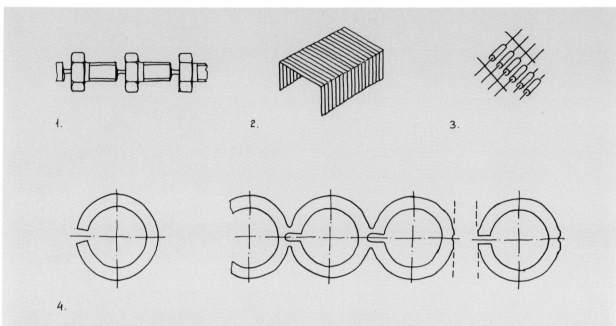

Components in bandform: (a) screws, (b) staples, (c) electrical components, (d) shows how a locking washer can be produced in bandform by means of redesigning.

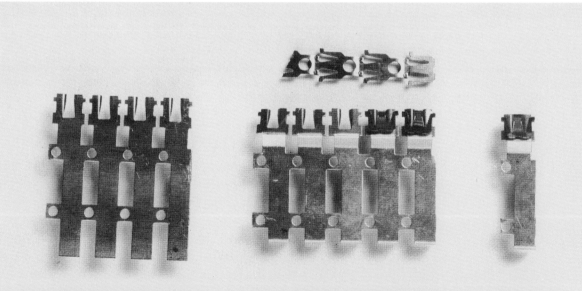

A sub-assembly composed of punched and bent band onto which is assembled a component which is correspondingly composed of punched and stamped band. Extreme right: the finished, sub-assembly which is cut free in the assembly machine. The components are part of an LK-NES switch, see examples on pages 81 and 123.

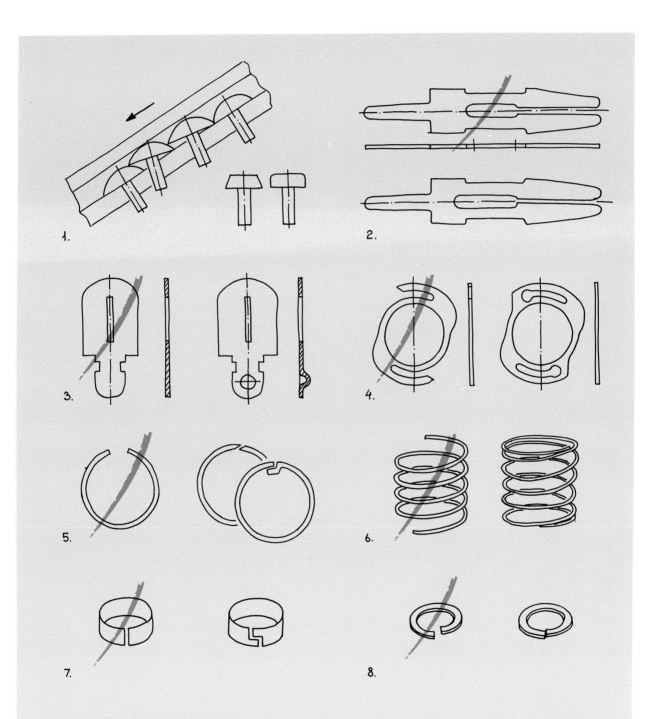

Some frequently-used-examples from literature. The second example demands an explanation: the wearing width is lessened so that is thinner than the thickness. Tangling is thus avoided.

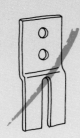  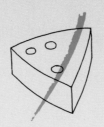 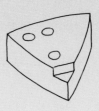

The subject in the example (a) is difficult to orientate, therefore it is supplied with a hanger that permits orienting and transport on a rail. Example (b) shows a subject which is oriented after the holes, which are not complemented by details in the other shape. A non-functional shoulder permits proper orientation to be established in a vibratory bowl feeder.

The orientation mark on this component for the Lego man is painted on. Light sensors are used in the vibration bowl feeder, and wrongly oriented components are blown back into the feeder with compressed air. The mark cannot be seen in the finished figure.

Avoid bad quality components   (Principle 8.6)

Distortions will cause tangling in mechanical or automatic equipment and can result in machine stoppage. In addition to a close scrutiny of the quality, as well as of surfaces and tolerations, one must ensure that the amount of distortions remains as small as possible.

The examples show various types of distortions.

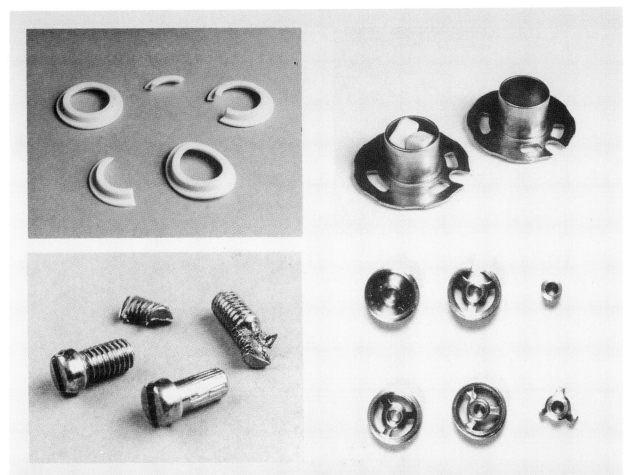

(a) Incomplete and broken plastic rings. (b) Subject with jammed stones from deburring. (c) Incomplete screws. (d) Incomplete special screws for gas valve.

A great deal of imagination is not required to envisage the damage that these could create in automatic assembly equipment.

Make the components symmetrical   (Principle 8.7)

The more symmetries the subject contains the fewer orientations are required. Principle 8.8 is to be used if absolute symmetry cannot be obtained: increase asymmetry.

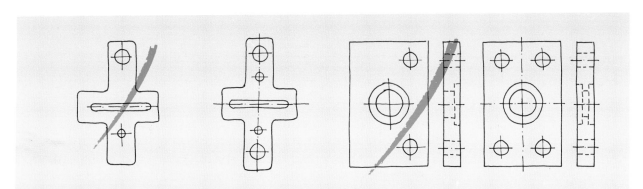

Two subjects where symmetry facilitates orienting.

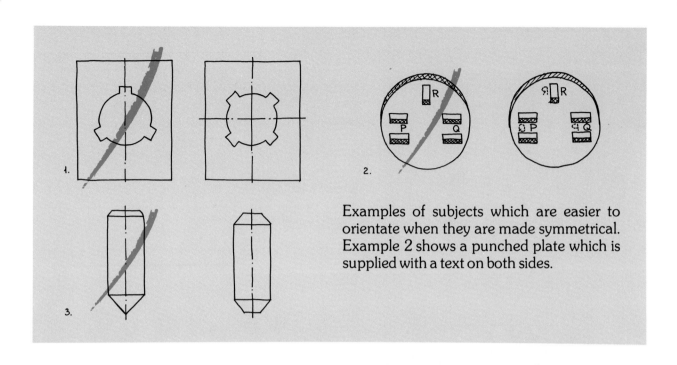

Examples of subjects which are easier to orientate when they are made symmetrical. Example 2 shows a punched plate which is supplied with a text on both sides.

Increased asymmetry (Principle 8.8)

If the components are almost symmetrical it becomes difficult for both assembler and the mechanical equipment to orientate the components. In this case full symmetry should be the goal (see 8.7), or the asymmetry should be clearly defined. In asymmetry there are possibilities for orienting the components with passive mechanisms based on, for example, the position of the centre of gravity, tendencies to turn or rotate etc.

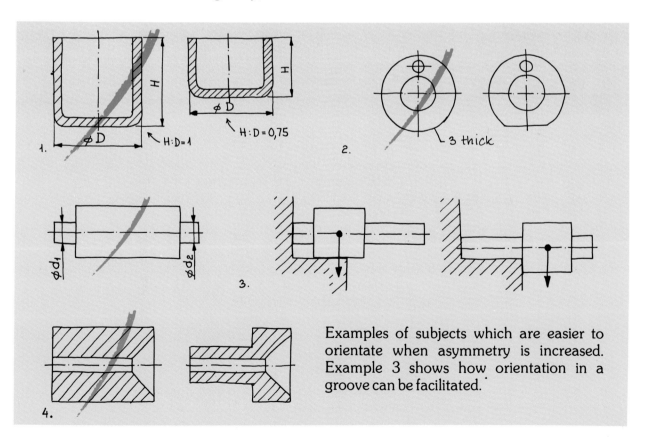

Examples of subjects which are easier to orientate when asymmetry is increased. Example 3 shows how orientation in a groove can be facilitated.

By "transport' one does not only refer to passive transport in grooves/chutes, cards/channels/rails etc., but also to transport in moving systems (e.g. pick-and-place units). General guidelines cannot be supplied as the movement takes place in so many different ways. General problems however, are shingling and wedging of components.

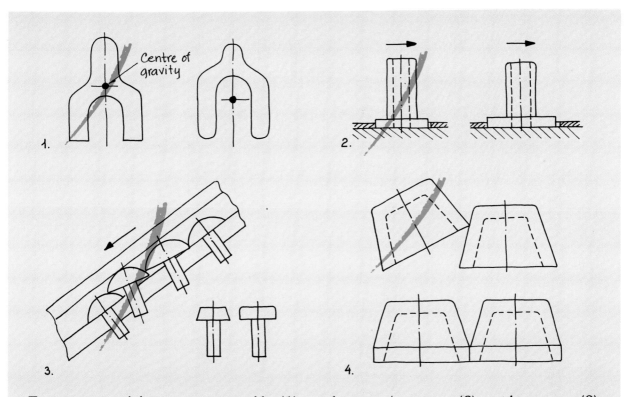

Transport possibilities are increased by (1) avoid tipping/capsizing; (2) avoid turnover; (3) permit rail transport; (4) avoid shingling.

This principle is discussed under structure principles, (Section 7.8, page 111), but will be further explained in greater detail. By "base" component is meant a larger component which comfortably allows itself to be transported from station to station in assembly. Generally one must strive to obtain:

– that the base component has many assembly surfaces common to the other components.

– that the largest number of joinings possible can be conducted directly, i.e. without having to keep to certain assembly sequences and conditions.

141

- that suitable attachment and support surfaces are available.

- that joining movements shall only be vertical or horizontal.

- that it is not necessary to turn the base component on the way.

These points are illustrated in the following:

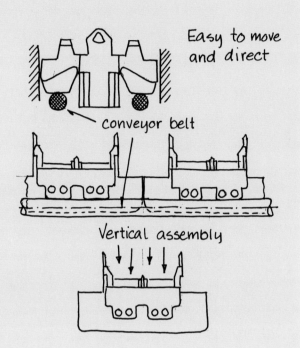

Basic unit from LK-NES switch. The components are easily moved and directed, many components in the row stabilise each other – and all assembly is executed from above. Compare with example on page 123.

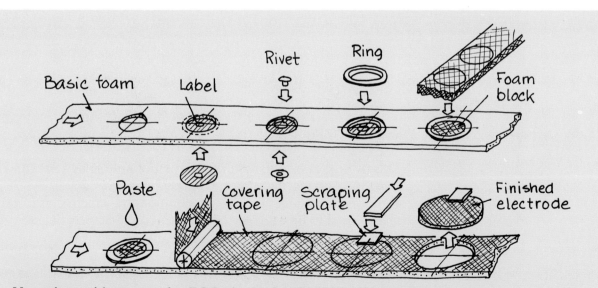

Untraditional base unit for ECG electrode (IPU). Plastic foam with the protective paper constitute simultaneously transport system and base unit for assembly (vertical from both sides). See example in section 9.4.

By simple patterns of movement is meant uncomposed linear movements. One should therefore avoid movements in various directions and curved movements.

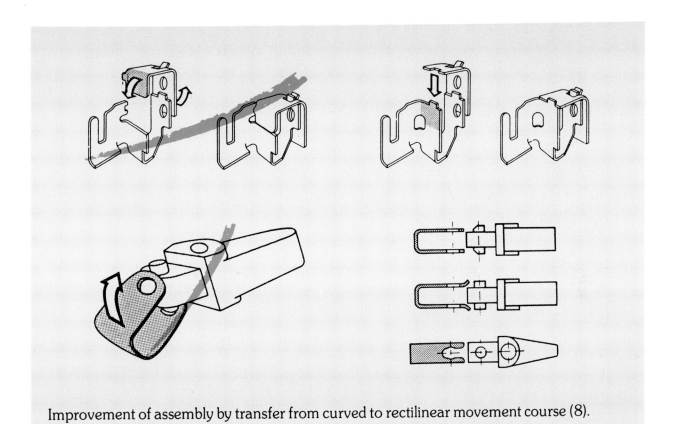

Improvement of assembly by transfer from curved to rectilinear movement course (8).

This basic part of a signal switch contains, as discussed on page 123, excellent solutions from the assembly point of view. The assembly of the spring strap however, is difficult as it must be executed by means of a curved movement through a small hole. The design is therefore suitable only for manned assembly. (LK-NES)

One should avoid the situation whereby various components or various details of one component must be placed simultaneously. If the situation cannot be avoided, one should design the components with requisite guide surfaces and/or elasticity.

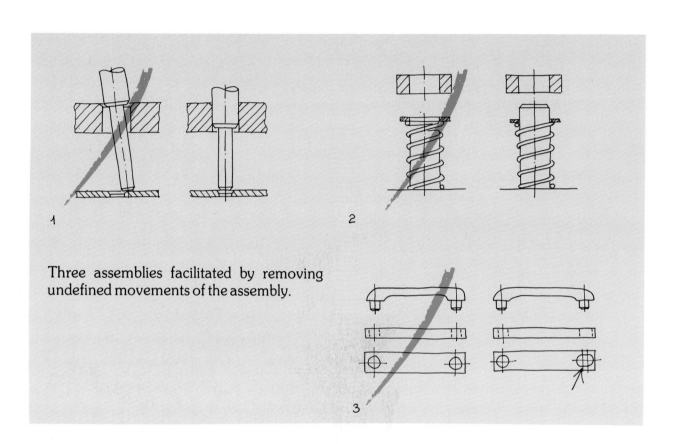

1

2

Three assemblies facilitated by removing undefined movements of the assembly.

3

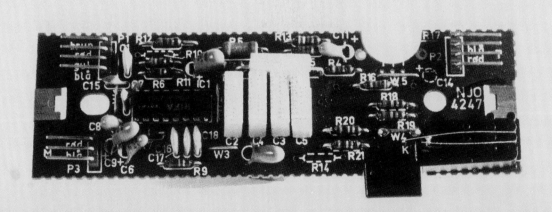

Print to be placed in the receiver of GNT Automatic telephone. The assembly on two cylindrical pins is facilitated by making one of the holes oblong.

Guide surfaces are those which help the component into place. They can be fitted to both mating units and they can also form part of an assembly fixture.

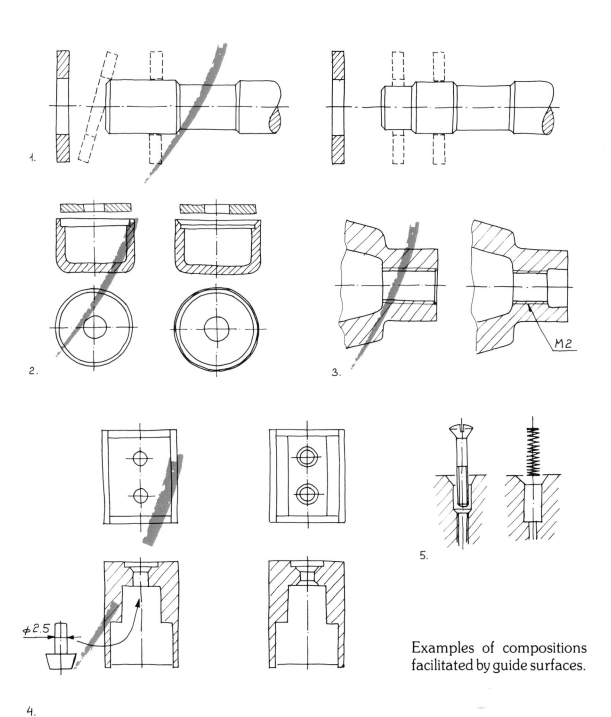

Examples of compositions facilitated by guide surfaces.

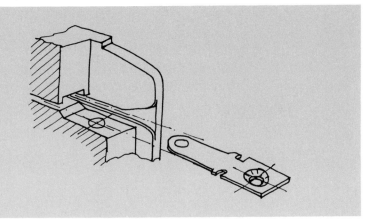

Abundant guide surfaces on a Danfoss contact for manual and planned automatic assembly. When the component is almost in place it is wedged with the aid of small bent flaps.

8.4 Review

The assembly principles discussed in this chapter are grouped below. Some of them have been covered in section 7.5, but they can also be regarded as belonging to the principles of component design.

In many of the examples (line drawings) in this chapter the references are lacking. These examples have been taken from (10) and (11).

PS: An example of a component is shown on page 129 where attention has not been paid to design for ease of assembly. Attempt to compare that component with the principles stated in this section.

COMPONENT DESIGN FOR EASE OF ASSEMBLY

PRINCIPLES:

Avoid assembly operations:

8.1   – integrate one component with another
7.16   – use integrating production methods

Avoid ORIENTATION:

8.2   – use magazines
8.3   – use components in the form of a band
7.16   – integrate production in assembly

Facilitate ORIENTATION:

8.4   – avoid tangling/nesting
8.5   – design special orientation surfaces
8.6   – avoid bad-quality components
8.7   – make the components symmetrical
8.8   – increase asymmetri

Facilitate TRANSPORTATION:

8.9   – make the components transport suitable
8.10   – design a base component

Facilitate INSERTION:

8.11   – choose simple moving pattern
8.12   – make insertion unambiguous
8.13   – fit the components with guide surfaces

Choose the correct JOINING METHOD:

7.14   – avoid joins
7.15   – avoid separate joining elements
7.16   – use integrating production methods

How is the assembly of these London buses different from the assembly of the real buses? Why?

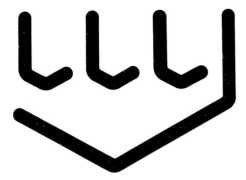

9

Integrated product development

SUMMARY

In this chapter we will turn our attention to designing for ease of assembly, partly as a rational (methodic) and partly as an integrated operation. The recognition and exploitation of design degrees of freedom is a salient point in this context.

An integrated approach to design goes hand in hand with an integrated perception of product development. Integration at this high level of abstraction is of paramount importance if one is to achieve comprehensive rationalisation of assembly.

Various principles for rationalisation can be applied – we have chosen five; their application in certain project situations is debatable but their importance in obtaining a good result is undeniable.

Rationalisation activities must be planned and controlled. A survey of the most influential factors in the field of assembly follows.

9.1 Procedure for design for ease of assembly

In chapters five to eight we have examined various principles which can lead to rational assembly results. They range from the project's assembly goal, the determination of the product programme, structural deliberations, to aspects of component design.

All this begs the question: "How is design for ease of assembly to be carried out?" How does one apply the principles in practice?

This we will attempt to answer by examining assembly problems on various levels, starting with design activity.

A methodical design process

Assembly problems have traditionally been regarded as product-orientated, to be solved during the production process; the same view applies to manufacturing processes. Research has shown however that the important decisions concerning production and assembly are taken during the design period, see Fig. 9.1. This results in 70% of the product's costs being determined during the design phase and only 20% during the actual production – in other words it is too late to deal with processes and assembly after the drawings and lists of parts have been completed. The need for an integrated approach is manifest.

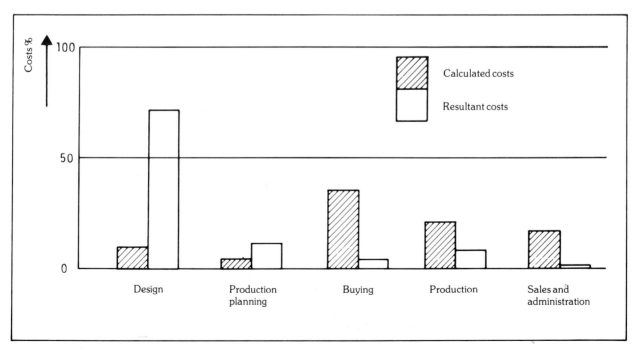

Fig. 9.1. Illustrates a typical cost distribution – both calculated and created – among a firm's departments. Note the lion's share of the cost is attached to product design.

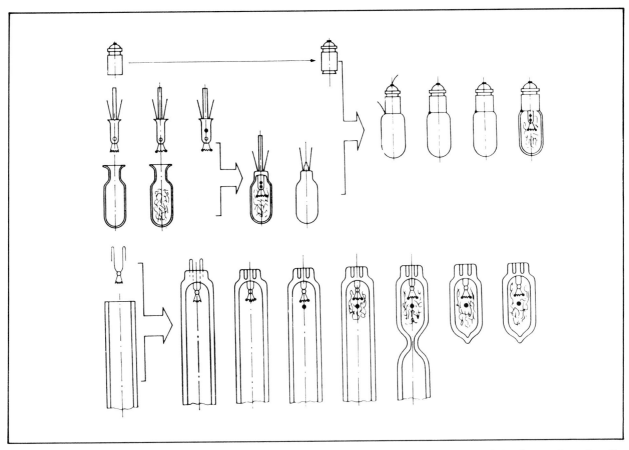

Fig. 9.2. Various designs can lead to the required function. Two different flash bulbs with radically differing production processes illustrate this. The lower is considerably easier to automate than the one above (15).

Fig 9.2 illustrates the implications when the designer determines the product. Consciously or otherwise he fixes process and production equipment also. A design strategy where product design, development, method planning and capacity and time planning follow in sequence is therefore not recommended.

Fig. 9.3 illustrates an ideal process, realisation of which, however, is difficult to achieve. Product and production equipment enjoy an integrated design. The figure shows the customary systematic steps, main functions, sub-functions and means and quantitive structure. The product's components are determined in branch form in order to accommodate not only standard components but also the total form plus the form of elements. Form division and integration plays a central role, an activity which leads to a detailed determination of the product's description (compare with structuring principles 7.3 and 7.4 in Chapter 7).

Two further activities run parallel to these, namely examination of manufacturing processes and examination of assembly processes. When these have been determined the production system can be designed simultaneously with the product's design.

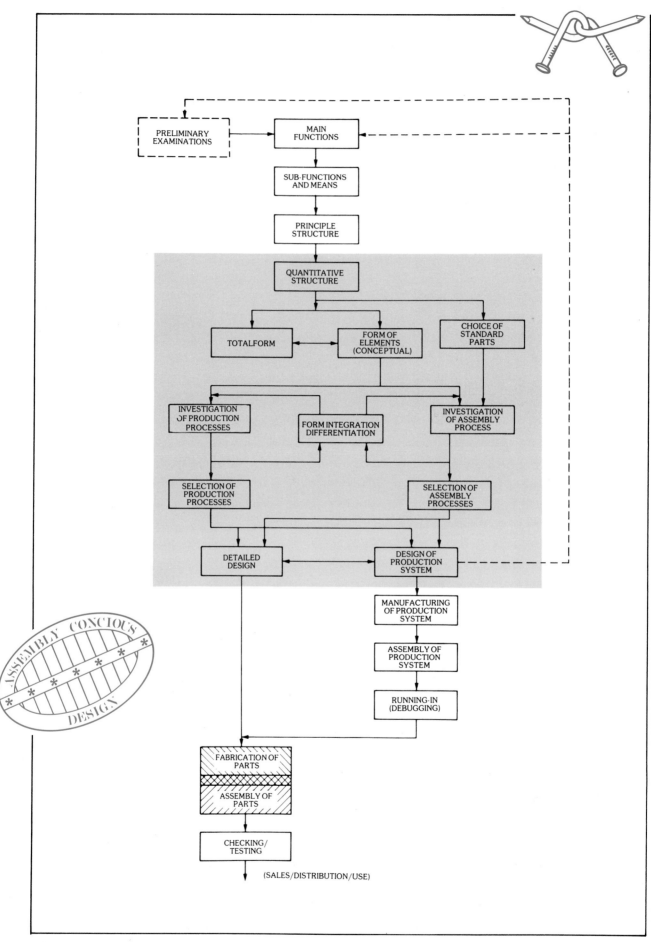

Fig. 9.3. The ideal procedure for integrated design. Partly after (4).

Create design degrees of freedom

The systematic procedure in Fig. 9.3 indicates the manifold levels on which alternatives can be created. These alternatives are necessary in order to achieve the optimal solution. The quality of a single solution cannot be verified.

The principles of design for ease of assembly can be used to create such alternatives which in turn respect these principles. The optimal solution can then be attained through an evaluation of the relevant criteria.

An important concept here is the recognition of "design degrees of freedom". One is traditionally loath to search for alternatives on various levels, secure in the feeling that one has already achieved the satisfactory solution.

Each of the boxes in Fig. 9.3 represents a level which, with the aid of variation methods, various degrees of freedom can be exploited. Variation of form division and integration is of considerable importance here, though often overlooked. The following example illustrates design variations for the structure of a pump.

9.2 Case Study: oil pump

The structuring of an oil pump is a part of the project where the goal is to produce a new generation of pumps. The basis is a pump design, complemented by working sketches and a functional model. Fig. 9.4 illustrates the pump's structure.

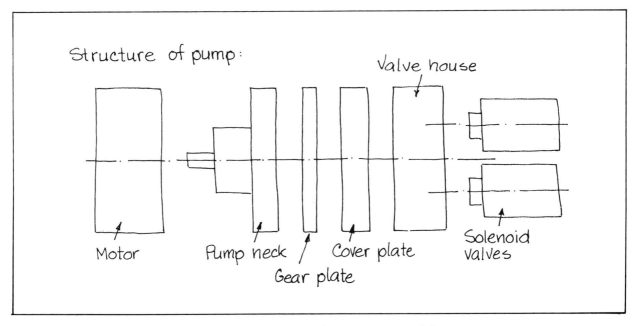

Fig. 9.4. The project's starting point: the structural composition of the pump.

Using this structure as a starting point, the requirement is a quantitative structure which:

- allows realisation of a large variety of function and design alternatives;

- leads to a product where function and production complement each other to such an extent that a satisfactory function can be achieved at the lowest production cost;

- which should be optimal with regard to choice of material, component design, processing, assembly, adjusting, checking and testing.

It is difficult to conceive the inclusion of all these in a project where the object is the revision of the pump's principles. Therefore we have chosen a pump project where new design is based on established principles. However, the principles for auxiliary functions (i.e. valves, packaging and shaft packing) are "open" – there exist design degrees of freedom which can complement the design of the pump as a whole.

A good example of this is the exploitation of design degrees of freedom on the structuring level as the requirements cannot be satisfied by a selection from existing component design.

Two starting points spring to mind. Firstly how does one create variations in principle and secondly, the search for a series of structural variations.

Brainstorming on the creation of variations produced:

- Exclude components, e.g. ABCDE/ABDE/ABCE . . .

- mount alternative components, e.g. $ABCD_1/ABCD_2$ . . .

- alter model plate (allowing uniformity of variation with unexploited functions).

- turn components, e.g. ABCD/∀BCD/ ⋗BCD . . .

- insert a program plate (a component without actual functions), e.g. foil with punched holes which determines functions.

- use variant-producing process in assembly, e.g. drill channel connections, stop holes.

The creation of structural variants can be tackled in different ways. One could imagine starting with a minimum of components and attempt to distribute their functions, gradually increasing them. Another systematic procedure would be to examine the number of gaskets and incorporate structures with one, two or three gaskets.

Brainstorming was the method employed in finding alternatives. The proposals illustrated were attained with the addition of some systematic supplements.

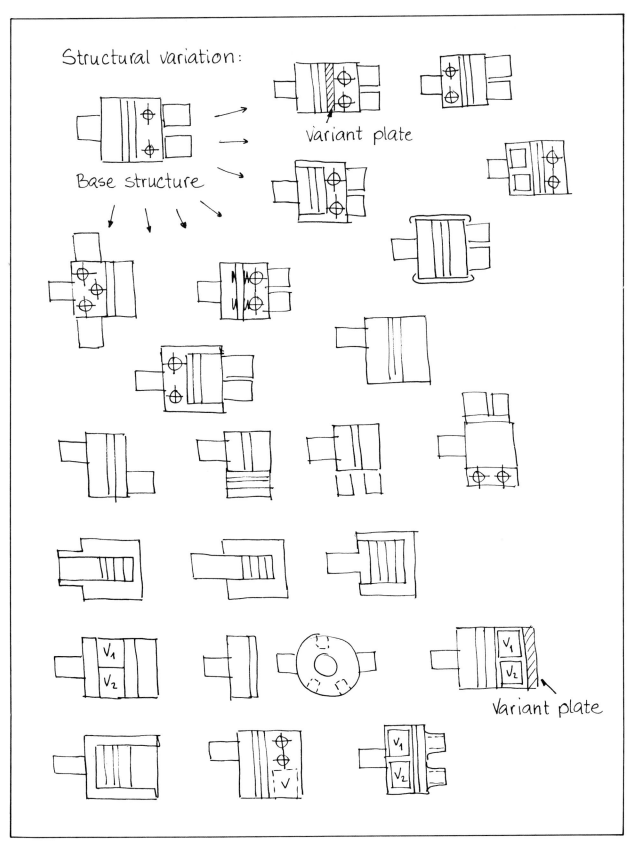

Fig. 9.5. Structured variation resulted in these alternatives, some of which can act as a basis for design for assembly.

The following criteria must be applied when examining proposed solutions:

- can it be done? Can functions, channels and variants be realised?

- Assembly: Can gradual automisation be achieved? Are the basic components suitable? Can variants be subsequently altered? Are there few parts? Are there expensive "variant remains" in the components?

- Testing: Are part and step by step testing possible? Are faults easily repairable?

- Processes: Are there few single parts? High tolerance? Few fixtures – few adjustments? Established technique.

- Materials: available, cheap?

This rough list of criteria gives an indication of how and to what extent the proposed solutions can be detailed. The sketched solutions cannot be evaluated using these criteria as they are not detailed enough. However, a comparison of the solutions is beneficial.

Four-man teams from production and design examined each solution in turn; four of their more detailed proposals are illustrated below.

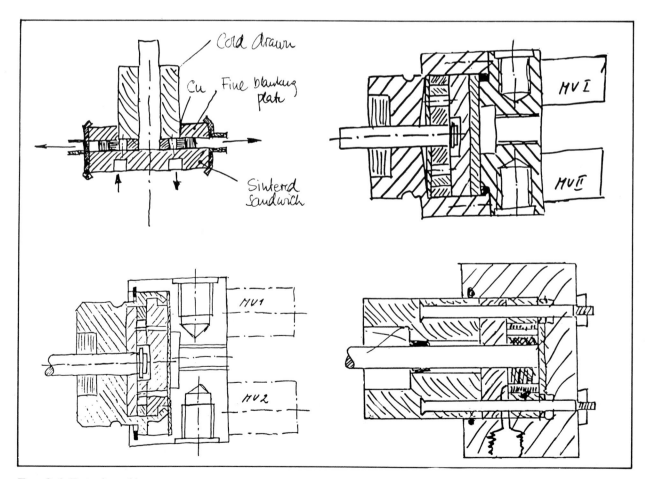

Fig. 9.6. Results of brainstorming concerning process-oriented design of structural alternatives.

The result was a series of ideas for further consideration and an indication of which ideas were worth pursuing.

The next step was systematic examination of five structural principles in order to ascertain and exploit design degrees of freedom). One considered a "role distribution" in a structure – that is allowing a component to contain various functions. The number of gaskets were included as leakage is a central problem. The result was five detailed sketches of pump models.

The above-mentioned criteria cannot immediately be applied to these five pumps – details of processing and assembly are lacking. Consequently two pumps were submitted to the product committee of the firm concerned, see photos beneath.

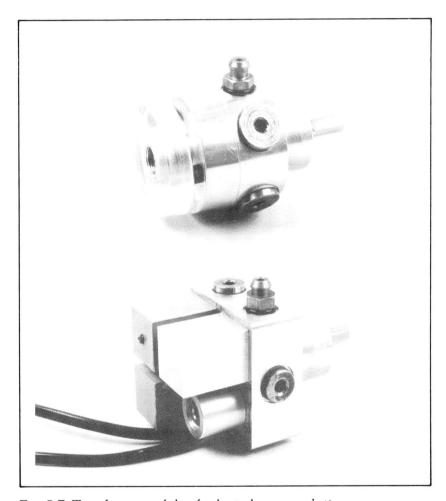

Fig. 9.7. Two form models of selected pump solutions.

9.3 Integrated product development

As idealistically illustrated in Fig. 9.3, the simultaneous determination of the form of the product (design) and the production process is desirable, however the responsibility is in practice divided between two parts of the organisation: the design and the production departments.

The high level of prices and wages in Denmark make it absolutely essential to rationalise the most important cost determining factors – fabrication and assembly. An important instrument for this purpose is the integration or simultaneous definition of product and process referred to above. A generalisation and extension of the integration problem to cover marketing, design and production is shown in Fig. 9.8. The area of integration in which there are important possibilities for rationalisation of the assembly process is illustrated in the figure: the dark area indicates rationalisation at the component and assembly equipment level, the intermediate area indicates rationalisation at the product structure and assembly process level, while the pale area shows potential rationalisation at the level of the project, product range, product type and choice of process.

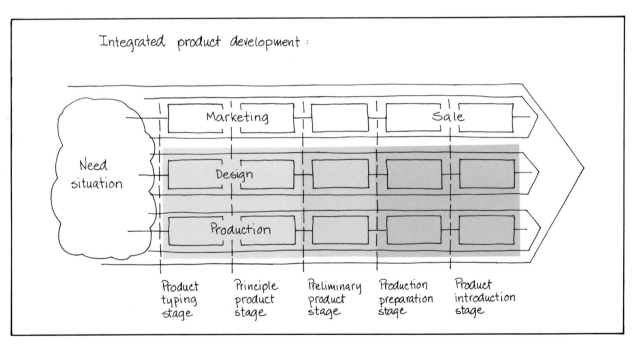

Fig. 9.8. Model describing an integrated project development.

Most projects – and the most common rationalisation efforts – lie within the dark area, but the greatest possibilities for rationalisation (and the greatest risk for the project) lie in the pale area.

Integrated product development implies an evaluation of the product based not only on marketing, design and product criteria, but also on an overall view of the criteria.

An example will now be presented of a project which contains essential features of the model in Fig. 9.8, in other words, an example of integrated product development.

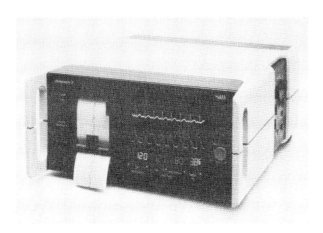

Fig. 9.9. S&W's latest apparatus for patient surveillance (photo S&W A/S).

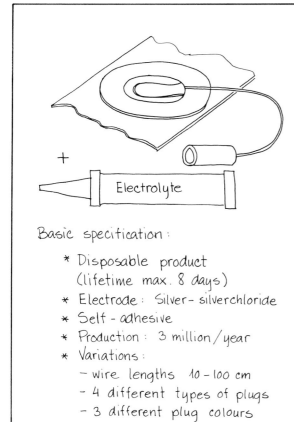

Basic specification:

* Disposable product
  (lifetime max. 8 days)
* Electrode: Silver-silverchloride
* Self-adhesive
* Production: 3 million/year
* Variations:
  - wire lengths 10-100 cm
  - 4 different types of plugs
  - 3 different plug colours

Fig. 9.10. The product as originally proposed. Note that the requirement as to variations concerns the wire and plug and not the actual electrode. Variants can therefore be completely avoided.

9.4 Case study: the ECG electrode

This example refers to a development project which the Institute for Product Development (IPU) carried out for the company Simonsen & Weel A/S (S&W). The project is an example of the integrated development of a product, a production technology and a production system.

The background for the project is that S&W produce and sell electronic equipment for patient surveillance, Fig. 9.9. A so-called ECG electrode is used as the pickup for the small electric currents produced by the functioning of the heart. When the project was started, S&W were buying their electrodes from an American firm, while they produced the electronic equipment themselves.

S&W were actually selling the product at the start of the project. In order to increase their profit margin, however, S&W decided to produce ECG electrodes themselves. The product which S&W wished to produce is shown in Fig. 9.10. As S&W wanted IPU to deliver fully automatic equipment for production of this product, IPU carried out a rapid analysis of the proposal.

Analysis of the proposed product

An analysis of the product of Fig. 9.10 gave the result:

★ The properties of the product as a measuring instrument would probably be excellent.

★ Improvements could be made in the way that the product is used. For example, it could be filled with electrolytic paste during production, so that the nurse does not need to do this.

★ The cost of materials in the product could probably be reduced.

★ The product's form is based on experience with manual production and is not well-chosen for fully automatic production. The many variations, for example, would be very troublesome.

On the basis of this analysis, IPU suggested starting a project, but that a step backwards should be taken so that the product became a variable.

159

Formulation of the task

The object of the project was therefore formulated as follows:

The principal aim of the project is to develop a new commercial opening for S&W in the field of disposable ECG electrodes. This aim is to be attained by integrated (parallel) evolution of the following tasks:

- ★ Development of a new ECG electrode.

- ★ Development of a production technology for fully automatic mass production.

- ★ Development, design, commissioning and delivery of a fully automatic production system.

The formulation gives the necessary *constuctive degrees of freedom* for an attempt to *optimise* S&W's commercial possibilities.

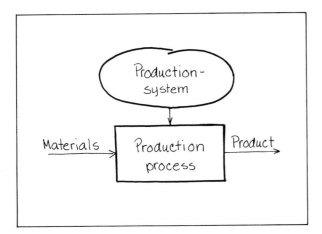

Fig. 9.11. A simple version of a project model.

A very simple model of the project is shown in Fig. 9.11. Note that the project really consists of two projects, which are carried out simultaneously: A "horizontal" project, which has as its outcome the product, and a "vertical" project, its outcome the production system. The two projects meet in the production process. Thus the development of this process plays a central role in the overall project. The two sub-projects are, as it happens, of very different types. One of them is to result in a product which is to be mass-produced. The other is a project whose result is a product (a machine) to be produced on a one-off basis.

160

Analysis of competitors

A comprehensive analysis of the competitors' products showed that:

- ★ The competing products are all badly packaged. The packing is expensive, and inconvenient to use. For example, the electrodes are often packed individually in aluminium foil bags, which are placed in a disorderly manner in a plastic bag. (Possibility of improvement.)

- ★ Several competitors use an electrode body consisting of a solid silver pin. The price of this is about half the total price of the materials for the product. From a functional point of view, a silver layer about 0.01mm thick, and thus requiring a very small amount of silver, is satisfactory. (Possibility of improvement.)

- ★ Those electrodes which are best from a functional point of view (that is to say, for making measurements with) are the worst from the point of view of production technique. They have too many components and too complicated a structure. (Possibility of improvement.)

- ★ The designs which are best with respect to production technique (few components, simple structure) are functionally the worst. (Possibility of improvement.)

- ★ The market for disposable electrodes is in a state of rapid expansion. Sales figures are rapidly rising, and the sales price must be expected to fall sharply. (Take note: The expected sales price for the new product will possibly be significantly altered even within the lifetime of this project.)

- ★ The market is expanding in the direction of pre-filled electrodes, where the electrode is filled with electrically conducting paste during the production process. The trend is thus towards a type of product other than that shown in Fig. 9.10, which would probably already be obsolete by the end of the project.

Experiments showed that:

- ★ With pre-filled electrodes there are

serious corrosion problems (if silver consumption is minimised), owing to the high concentration of chloride ions in the conducting paste, the most obvious way to minimise the use of silver is by galvanic coating of a base material with a thin layer of silver. The only practical solution was to try to coat a plastic component with a very thin layer of silver. The corrosion problem meant it was essential for there only to be silver and no other metals present in the coating process. A technology of this type was unknown at the time. Many time-consuming experiments had to be made before the required technology was successfully developed.

The result is, that the body of the electrode contains only as much silver as is required for measurement purposes. Mechanical strength in the electrode body is provided by the plastic component.

Strategy and financial considerations

As the aim of the project was to create the most profitable commercial possibility for S&W, it is necessary to consider the development project not just as a matter of manipulating technical factors, but to a considerable extent also one of manipulating economic factors, as shown in Fig. 9.12. As can be seen from the figure, each technical factor has financial consequences. Only by simultaneous adjustment of both the product, the production process and the technical properties of the equipment and by trying to convert the technical properties into economic consequences, is it possible to achieve the establishment of the most profitable commercial possibility.

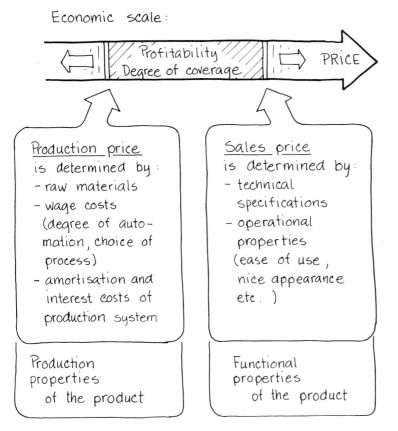

Fig. 9.12. The aim of the project is to create the most profitable commercial possibilities, i.e. to maximise the degree of coverage. This is done by manipulating the properties of the product, so as to obtain the greatest possible sales price for the least possible production price. Notice that both the product's manufacturing properties and its functional properties can be manipulated. All too often only the functional properties (determined by the market) are altered. The result is that the production department are left with task problems that should not exist.

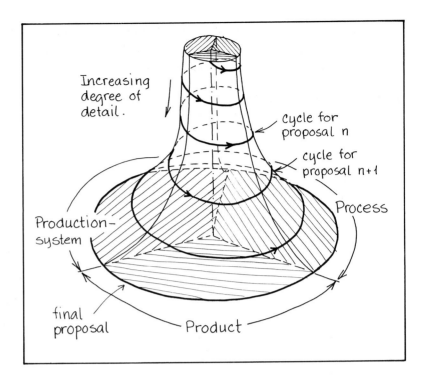

Fig. 9.13. During the project, a large number of different proposals were examined. Each proposal was a combination of the form of the product, in conjunction with production technology and an outline for a plant. After a number of iterations, the relationships between the three variables begin to be stabilised, so that an optimum, balanced combination is attained.

Normally integrated product development will also involve development of the market. This activity was not very prominent in the current project since the market had already been developed in connection with S&W's sale of an American manufactured electrode.

The project strategy is an iterative process, as illustrated in Fig. 9.13. A large number of alternatives are investigated. Each alternative consists of proposals for the form of the product, the production technology and the production plant. The individual cycles of this process are characterised by continual rejection of proposals which have shown themselves to be less advantageous, together with a continually increasing degree of details.

Proposals regarding the product

At the same time as the analysis of competitors is carried out, a long series of proposals concerning the product itself is worked out. A proposal for a product, as it normally appears from the drawings, is principally characterised by:

- The design (structure)
- The form of the components
- The number of components
- The choice of materials.

Note: When these features have been determined – for example in the form of drawings – the material costs for the product can be calculated and its functional properties can be evaluated by production and testing of prototypes.

It is not, however, possible to determine whether its properties from the point of view of production are optimal. But even if the production properties cannot be determined from the drawings, they are nevertheless more or less completely determined at the time when the product is designed (drawn).

Proposals regarding the production process

For the most promising product proposals, one or more production processes were proposed, each characterised by:

- The manufacturing processes for the individual components
- Assembly processes
- Checking processes
- The processing sequence
- The form of the raw materials as delivered (as single components, in rolls, etc.)
- The pattern of movement of tools and other active elements
- The timing of the processes
- Buffer storage.

162

The various proposals were documented/sketched as shown in Fig. 9.16, and we were now well on the way to being able to evaluate the properties of the product with respect to its production, but we did not have a sketch of the production system at that time.

Proposals regarding the production system (machine + operator)

For the most promising production processes, proposals were made for alternative systems (both machines and operators), which could realise the production processes in question. Each system was characterised by:

- The operator's tasks
- The machine's tasks.

As it rapidly became apparent that it would be both technically possible and economically advantageous to have fully automatic production, the operator's tasks were reduced to:

- Supplying raw materials
- Removal of the finished products and packaging
- Fault correction
- Supervision.

The machine was characterised by:

- Its frame design
- The design of the tools
- The control system
- The checking system
- The feeding and orientation system for raw materials
- The storage system
- Its appearance
- The way in which it is operated
- The cycle time
- Its productivity
- Its flexibility (readjustment to other tasks)
- Its size
- Its weight.

These properties determine the performance (capacity, quantity) of the system, the cost of the machine and the direct wage costs for carrying out the actual production.

It is then possible to evaluate which combination of product construction, production technology and plant could provide S&W with the best commercial possibilities. The chosen combination will now be discussed.

The product

The resulting product is shown in Fig. 9.14. It is made up of nine components, of which all except two (the rivet and ballpart) are held together by adhesive.

Functional properties

The properties of the electrode as a measurement device are principally determined by the fact that the electrode body (denoted "the rivet" in Fig. 9.14) is of silver/silver chloride. This means that the signal specifications are just as good as those of the competing products. A selection of the properties of the electrode from the point of view of the user:

★ The electrodes all lie the same way round in their packaging and therefore always have the same orientation when they are taken hold of (Fig. 9.15).

★ The electrode is ready for use when opened, as this exposes a self-adhesive surface.

★ The electrode is attached to the patient by self-adhesion.

★ An electric wire from the measuring apparatus is attached by a snap lock (plug).

Note that alteration of the original system boundary for the product has made it possible to eliminate the requirement that variants should be produced. The wire and plug no longer belong to the disposable product, which results in a cheaper production system and reduced material costs.

Properties as regards production

These can most conveniently be deduced from the production process. They are only inferred on a drawing of the product (Fig. 9.14). Therefore it is very important to sketch the production process as a step in the definition of the product. It is precisely this which is one of the ideas in integrated product development.

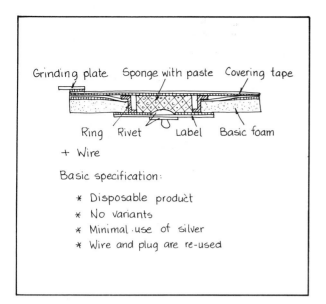

Grinding plate   Sponge with paste   Covering tape

Ring   Rivet   Label   Basic foam

+ Wire

Basic specification:

* Disposable product
* No variants
* Minimal use of silver
* Wire and plug are re-used

Fig. 9.14. The resulting product is made up of nine components. There are no variants of the electrode. The requirement that there should be variants is satisfied by the wire (which is the part in which variations are desired) which connects the electrode and the measuring apparatus being a re-usable product. This is not connected to the disposable product (the electrode) until it is to be used (snap lock connection). This offers advantages with respect to both production technique and economy (it eliminates the need for materials for the wire and plug).

Fig. 9.15. The electrode is packaged conveniently for use: The product sits a particular way round.

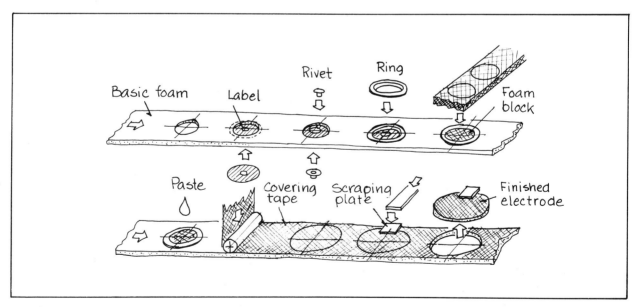

Fig. 9.16. The production process is the central link between the two sub-projects: development of the product and development of the automatic plant. Possible production processes were sketched as shown in the figure for a long series of product proposals. In this way, the consequences (properties) of a given proposal with respect to production technique can be evaluated, as the roughly drafted production process can easily and rapidly be transformed to a machine design in the machine designer's imagination or on his sketchpad. An iterative process which can lead to optimisation is thus initiated.

The production process

The resulting production process can be seen in Fig. 9.16. It is characterised by:

★ One of the components – the basic foam – is used as a base component on which the other components are mounted. This base component is in addition used as an integrated part of the machine's transport system, in that the tape from which the base component is produced is used as feeding mechanism, carrier tape and holding device. (Thus the base component does not appear as a separate component until the end of the production process when the electrode is stamped out).

★ The machine has been designed for fabrication of many of the components as possible, so that production and assembly can take place sequentially. This eliminates orientation operations, which tend to give serious reliability problems.

★ This means that the following components are fabricated in the machine from rolls of raw material, Fig. 9.17:

  – The base component (punching and stamping out)
  – The sponge (stamping out)
  – The covering tape (stamping out together with the electrode)
  – The scraping plate (clipping).

The consequence of this is:

  – Cheaper components

  – Greater reliability

★ Only three of the components – the rivet, ballpart and ring – have to be oriented.

★ Only the process stations associated with these components will encounter appreciable reliability problems.

★ Buffer storage between the process stations can therefore be omitted, thus reducing the machine's price and space requirements.

★ The pattern of movements is very simple:

  – All active tool movements are parallel and lie in the same vertical plane
  – The majority of components are fed forward horizontally
  – All active tool movements take place simultaneously and have the same stroke length, making it possible to use a very simple driving system, as shown in Fig. 9.19.

★ The components have forms which allow all fabrication operations (punching, stamping and clipping) to be performed using rotationally symmetrical tools, making it possible to use a very simple tool system, as shown in Fig. 9.18.

★ All variants have been eliminated, which means that adaptation to variants of the various sub-systems of the machine is unnecessary.

Fig. 9.17. Components can either be supplied to the automatic machine in bulk form (not oriented), or can be produced from rolls of material within the machine immediately prior to assembly. In this way, orientation operations can be eliminated.

Troichoid input has been chosen as far as possible, as illustrated.

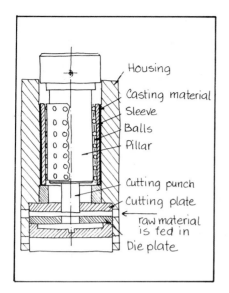
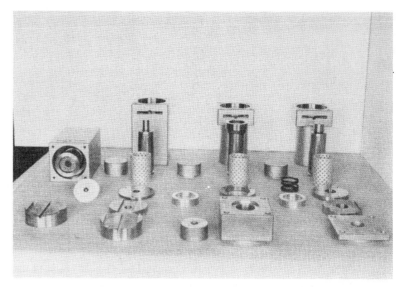

Fig. 9.18. With the available raw materials, there is a requirement that the cutting gap in the tools be only 0.005mm. By deliberately designing the components so that they can be produced by rotationally symmetrical tools, extremely precise tools can be produced very cheaply using an unconventional tool design which is the same for all four tools: The "expensive' components are bought as a standard pillar die unit consisting of a sleeve, ball cage and pillar. (High quality and precision for a reasonable price.) A hardening cutting punch made especially for the purpose is glued (small forces) into the pillar. In addition, a housing and a hardened die plate, whose hole matches the punch so as to give the desired cutting gap, are manufactured. After this, the tool is assembled and filled out with casting material (Araldite). The inconvenient and very costly chain of tolerance adjustments found in traditional tool designs is therefore eliminated. The tolerance requirements are thus not satisfied by very fine finishing (grinding), but by unconventional assembly.

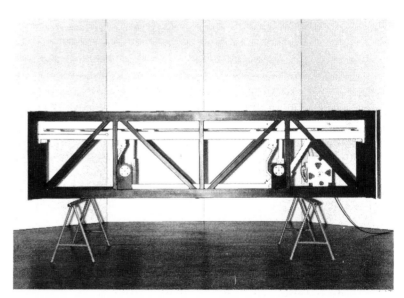

Fig. 9.19. This sequencing mechanism is driven by a single main motor and has the following functions: Operating the tools, mechanical control of tool movements and transport of the base material. When the crank of the mechanism has performed a revolution, all active tool movements have been performed with the required stroke length and the base material has been moved forward the required distance, all with the desired accelerations and at the required time. Thus movement and control are integrated. This simple system replaces about 18 pneumatic cylinders with their associated control systems. Furthermore it is practically noiseless.

Fig. 9.20. The machine has a capacity of three million units per year. Emphasis has been laid on an attractive appearance, even though it is a special machine of which only a single example is to be manufactured. If the operator is proud of his machine it will be looked after more carefully. In this way a pleasant working environment and high productivity are obtained simultaneously.

The production system

The production process is carried out using the automatic machine shown in Fig. 9.20. The machine is characterised by:

★ Being operated by a single unskilled operator.

★ Cycle time of 2 seconds.

★ A low stoppage rate is achieved by:
  – Choosing reliable principles for the way in which the machine's fabrication and assembly stations work.
  – Choosing a mechanical driving system with only one main motor, Fig. 9.19.
  – Choosing a mechanical control system, Fig. 9.19.
  – Integrated fabrication and assembly, so that orientation operations as far as possible are avoided, Fig. 9.21.

  – Specifying a uniform level of quality for the raw materials.
  – Making material rolls and storage containers as large as practicable, so that refilling with raw materials takes place as infrequently as possible and (if possible) with the machine running.
  – Arranging for the control panel to immediately indicate a stoppage, and which operation (feed process or raw material) is the reason for the stoppage, Fig. 9.22.
  – Making it possible to refill with raw materials on the fly or with the shortest possible down time. An automatic warning that refilling with raw materials is required aids this.
  – Protecting all stations and critical components against overload, so that breakdowns with consequent considerable periods of stoppage are avoided.

167

Fig. 9.21. In several of the automatic machines' stations, integrated fabrications and assembly takes place. These stations have a reliability several orders of magnitude better than those with feed and orientation of components delivered in bulk.

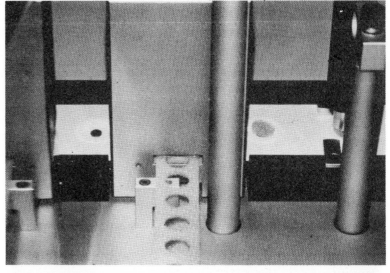

Fig. 9.22. The operation panel is the communication link between operator and machine. A simple and easily understood design is important for minimising the machine's down time.

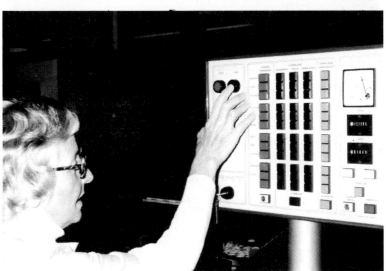

★ Short down time is achieved by the following:

- Certain components are checked before being fed in, so that assembly of faulty ones is avoided.
- All feed operations are checked so that incorrect assembly is avoided.
- All fabrication and assembly processes are checked so that any error does not propagate to the following stations with more work being required for re-establishment as a consequence.
- Before a cycle is started, a check is made that all raw materials for fabrication or assembly are present, so that empty "operations" – with subsequent manual rectification – are avoided.

- The machine is ready for operation immediately after the current has been switched on with the start key.

★ An attractive appearance was achieved by specifying the following design principles at a very early stage of the design:

- All surfaces of the frame construction are to be black.
- All cover panels are to be orange-red.
- All functional units are to be silvery (steel and brass are to be given a matt chrome surface, aluminium is to be anodised).

★ High quality in the final product is achieved by checking all working operations in the machine by means of an electronic control system.

Fig. 9.23. This model was extremely useful, for example for evaluation of the way in which the machine was operated. It could be made quickly and cheaply from available materials: a table, some chipboard and some blocks of plastic foam.

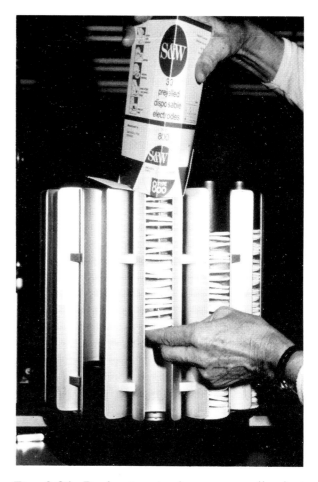

Fig. 9.24. Packaging is done manually, but rapidly and conveniently.

★ Good operating conditions were achieved by making a very simple full scale model of the machine from available parts (a table, a piece of chipboard, some blocks of plastic foam etc., Fig. 9.23) at a very early stage of the project.

★ The driving system and control system are integrated into one unit: a mechanism driven by a single motor, see Fig. 9.19.

★ The tool system is of an unusual design, in which high quality and low price are achieved simultaneously, Fig. 9.18.

★ A very low noise level is attained by:

  – Avoiding as far as possible the generation of noise, by choosing low-noise drive principles.

  – Preventing the propagation of noise, where it arises, e.g. in vibratory bowl feeders.

★ The electrodes are delivered to the operator with a well-defined orientation in a container with 30 electrodes in each tube, so that packaging can be conveniently performed. Thus the chosen form of packaging provides both a cheap package (materials, wages, equipment) and a high utility value for the customer, see Fig. 9.24.

Experiences with commissioning and production

Commissioning was very troublesome. This was chiefly due to the facts that:

169

★ Cheap raw materials were used in order to reduce material costs as far as possible. This philosophy was balanced by the consideration that the quality of the product should be as high as the best of the competitors. Several of the raw materials are in fact mass produced standard items which are manufactured for completely different applications.

★ The aim was to achieve fully automatic production and thus very low wages costs.

★ Bold ideas were incorporated into the machine – for example, the choice was made to omit the inclusion of buffer stores, even though the machine has a large number of stations.

★ IPU had no previous experience of the development of ECG electrodes or of systems for the mass production of these.

★ S&W had no previous experience of mass production.

★ Some of the electrode's components were to be produced using methods which were new to subcontractors and methods untested on an industrial scale. This was the case for the special silver coating of the electrode body.

★ The development work took place under extreme pressure owing to over-optimistic time schedules and budgets.

On the whole, the project's level of ambition was set much too high, however when things turn out right one is happy one took the risk, while if things go badly then everyone is suddenly able to see that the level of ambition has in fact been set too high. In this case everything luckily ran smoothly, even if commissioning was characterised by a large number of problems having to be solved.

After a trial production with the manufacture of half a million electrodes at IPU, with the machine being operated by personnel from S&W, the production system was moved to S&W, where it has since produced many millions of electrodes. It has now been replaced by a new, faster and more flexible machine, which S&W themselves have developed and designed on the basis of experience from the project discussed here. The system delivered by IPU has now been set up in the USA, where it is used for production under licence.

Conclusion

IPU feel that they have shown by means of this project that integrated product development is a suitable strategy for the establishment of an optimal commercial possibility. Simultaneous adjustment of the characteristics of the product, production process and system have the effects that:

★ *The total development time is reduced*
   The progress of the project will indeed apparently go slower at first, because problems which are traditionally kept until later are solved at a very early stage of the work. (Often it is true that the earlier problem is recognised and solved, the "cheaper" this can be done.)

★ *Development costs are reduced*

★ *A more profitable commercial opportunity is achieved*

9.5 Possibilities for rationalisation in a wider perspective

As we have seen in Chapter 1 an overwhelming need exists for a rationalisation of assembly.

Among the reasons for the relatively slow rationalisation in assembly compared to that of processing are:

★ Those human skills aided by sight and touch which a machine can only achieve with a great deal of difficulty.

★ The batch size is often too small and the number of variants too high.

★ Product life is often unfavourably compared to the payback period for automats.

★ Assembly machines are often produced for a specific product and are difficult to alter (hard automation), with the result that the firm's production programme flexibility is limited.

These factors can no longer be put forward as a serious basis for not attempting rationalisation of assembly. This is backed up by rising demand for higher wages, better working environment and greater competitiveness. They are only applicable where rationalisation in the form of automation has been contemplated. Fig. 9.25 illustrates a series of rationalisation possibilities.

Though this book concentrates on design for ease of assembly, it contains many principles which can be applied to a rationalisation outside the design area – e.g. in processing, handling, mechanising, automating, technology and organisation.

Principles of rationalisation

In Chapters 5 to 8 we have taken the liberty of describing guidelines for ease of assembly as principles, as we believe the technical relationship is synonymous. The situation is otherwise, however, when we turn to principles for rationalisation activity at a higher level. Here the salient principles are those of profitability. We will permit ourselves to formulate some principles applicable here, although undoubtedly managing directors will not agree with all of them.

POSSiBILITIES FOR RATIONALIZATION:

- New production processes
  - eliminate assembly
  - reduce the number of components

- New composing processes

- Simplify handling of components

- Integrate component production and assembly

- Assembly oriented design
  - module structure
  - integrated design and assembly

- Mechanization

- Automation

- Flexible automation

- New production principles
  - group technology

- New organization principles
  - within production
  - within product development

Fig. 9.25. Overall view of various possibilities for rationalisation. It is apparent that design-oriented assembly is not the only one.

We contend that it is important to present more provocative principles – if only to stimulate contemplation of existing ones.

Attempt not to pressure product development (Principle 9.1)

A new product containing new principles, processes and optimal assembly is rare, particularly if the development team is unaccustomed to radical steptaking. A thorough rationalisation of assembly processes should commence on the basis of an established product.

Pressurising the project start can ultimately cause problems (Principle 9.2)

Decisions which affect subsequent work are taken throughout the development project. Mistakes here can seldom be rectified by adjusting later phases of the project. If the start is pressurised (i.e. too hasty decisions) the result can be massive corrections later on.

A short development time is acceptable if the next generation is being planned (Principle 9.3)

The realisation that one cannot reach an optimal result in a short-term project can lead to another strategy where pressurising the project is tolerable – if the next generation is carefully planned – i.e. observe and document every facet of repetition, temporary solutions, incomplete measurements and considerations.

The initial assembly projects are unprofitable (Principle 9.4)

These require an extra effort particularly if the team is new to the technology. These additional costs in the design phase, product adaptation or running-in period can (unexpectedly) reduce profitability, but will pay dividends in subsequent projects, as a rule.

Accept longer depreciation period (Principle 9.5)

If one accepts that assembly rationalisation is inevitable, in order to achieve competitiveness; that countries such as Japan accept longer depreciation periods than is customary in Europe, then it is necessary to execute assembly rationalisation even though it is more expensive than other product related investments.

Assembly rationalisation is also a management problem (Principle 9.6)

This has been discussed in Principle 6.3 but is repeated here in order to emphasise that results should not only be expected in production preparation. If the effect is to be of consequence, an integrated effort is necessary.

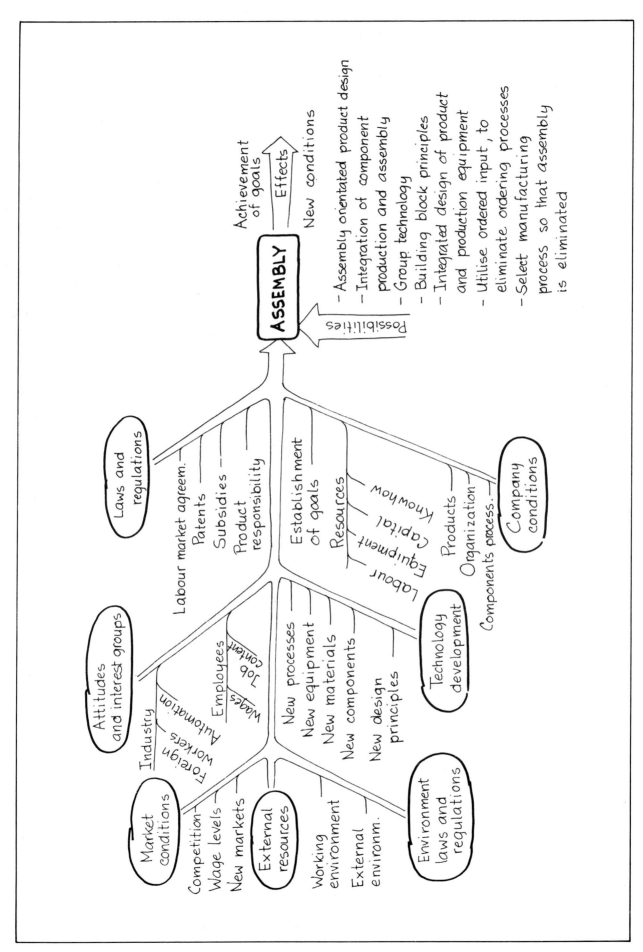

Fig. 9.26. A group of external factors which affect assembly development.

9.6 Formation of development plans

Assembly has claimed a steadily increasing share of total wages as a result of the relatively slow production technique development in the area over the past decades; this in stark contrast to developments in the area of component production.

Assembly is typically manual and accounts for between 40 and 60% of a product's time consumption. This in spite of assembly lines, division of labour and time and motion studies.

Increasing demands for greater job content, improved working environment and higher wages demand rationalisation if we are to compete effectively and increase production.

In the previous section we outlined various possibilities for rationalisation in addition to assembly-oriented design. The development of the assembly department must be consciously directed if the gains are to be tangible. Fig. 9.26 illustrates a group of factors which influence assembly function, some external, others which can be adopted to deal with or exploit these situation changes.

Development plans

The formation of such plans for assembly functions can be regarded as an attempt to govern development. Simultaneously the fruits of this can be regarded as a tool for both management and workforce. Here is a dynamic implement which must be kept up to date.

IPU has carried out such a task for a large Danish firm. The establishment of development plans is listed below:

1. Analysis of the existing product assortment, key cost figures and assembly methods. (The work is carried out in conjunction with the client and partly on his premises.) Possible future products are included in the analysis.

2. Localising of those products wholly or partly suited to automatic assembly.

3. Formation of alternative assembly methods for these.

4. Development plans for the products suited to automatic assembly. The plans contain:

    4.1 Survey of products and their characteristics.

    4.2 Proposals for assembly equipment, including assembly machines.

    4.3 Survey of assembly machines suppliers.

    4.4 Schedule for realisation of programme.

    4.5 Evaluation of consequences in relation to investment,

profitability, quality control, working environment, staffing, etc.

5. Establishment of guidelines for module construction of assembly machines tailored to these products.

The process was decisively implemented by the fact that automatic assembly was required. Similar considerations can be applied however to the introduction of gradual manual assembly or a transformation to highly automated or flexible systems.

Development tendencies - Conclusions

SUMMARY

Rising wages and increasing demands to the working environment will have the effect of raising the degree of automation of assembly in the future.

The future assembly lines will have fewer stations and larger buffer stores. This will bring about better working conditions as well as reducing sensitivity towards absence and disturbances.

Future products will be designed through co-operation between the design and production departments.

A number of difficult assembly processes will be eliminated by means of selection of other methods of production.

As a result of the wish to automate assembly even in the case of small batch sizes, experiments will be carried out with flexible assembly systems.

177

10.1 The future

The subject of assembly technique was dealt with in "Jernets Fremtidsprojekt" (14) in 1979. That material is not obsolete – the summary can be applied fully to today's situations.

We have chosen to print the summary here in full, to make additions on a few points, and from this to come to a conclusion about the role of this book within the assembly field.

The situation today

In Danish industry as well as industry abroad, assembly is generally carried out manually and represents between 40 to 60% of the total production time. When these figures are compared to our level of wages it means that competition from those countries with a low wage level is tough, especially for those products with a relatively high wage quota in assembly.

Up until now competitiveness has just about been maintained by means of steadily increasing productivity. The increase in productivity is often achieved by application of the assembly line principle, division of work and methods related to time and motion studies, and thus has been achieved significantly by a striving for an optimal utilisation of the human labour force. The result is that in many cases the operator's work has lacked content and become monotonous, with frequent, repetitive movements resulting in both physical and psychological problems.

It can be expected therefore that significant changes will take place in the assembly field in the coming years, on account of both competitiveness and working environment.

When compared to the processing field which has achieved great increases in productivity in recent years, the assembly field has only undergone minor changes.

Endeavours to achieve automation are often hindered by the fact that product construction and component design take place without taking automation into account. A product's assembly and a significant part of the problems attached to it are in fact determined in its design. But it has been customary up until now for designers to concern themselves first and foremost with the product's function, then with the component's function, and only minimally with assembly.

Automation is sharply limited – from the financial point of view – in the cases of small batch size and many variations.

Situation and conditions in the coming 10-15 years

★ Rising wages and increasing demands to the working environment will have the effect that the degree of mechanisation and automation will increase sharply.

The application of the assembly line principle can often result in the achievement of high productivity, but this is often attained at cost to the operator's working station, which becomes trivial, tempo-dominated and provides no opportunities for personal expression and development. It can be expected that the assembly line principle will come in for increasing criticism from the employee's side. In order to deal with this criticism, and also to increase flexibility and lessen quality problems, new forms of organisation will gain ground.

★ A sharply increasing number of assembly operations will be executed in independent (autonomous) production groups.

★ The assembly line of the future will contain fewer stations and larger buffer stores so that the following can be achieved simultaneously: more satisfactory working conditions, greater flexibility and reduced sensitivity to absence and disturbances.

In the fields of assembly for single pieces and small batches, progress during the next 10-15 years will probably also be small and be concentrated on better tools and improved design of the place of work.

Flexible programmable assembly equipment such as robots and numerically controlled assembly machines are increasing and will continue to increase their numbers on the market. Their area of application is, however, limited to those tasks where orientation operations are not involved.

★ Robots will normally be used in assembly for:
   (1) Handling of tools. Examples are: spot welding, arc welding and spray painting.
   (2) Handling of components which are oriented.

Automatic orientation of components presents difficulties of a high degree, since automatic, flexible equipment is lacking. An effective possibility is however, to take advantage of the fact that the components being processed often have a well-defined orientation. This can occur in two ways:

★ The components will increasingly be delivered ready for assembly. This can be achieved with the aid of processed bands, tape, fixtures, magazines, packaging, etc.

★ The integration of component production and assembly will, in certain areas, be increased.

179

In the realm of large batches and mass production, where one or more products are produced in large numbers over a long period, favourable conditions for automation exist. Assembly is still carried out manually to a high degree and assembly automats are used only to a limited extent. However in the years to come one may expect:

★ Assembly machines in the fields of large batches and mass production will achieve increasing flexibility of application and will represent an effective means of rationalisation and attainment of greater job content. Such equipment will be especially produced for a specific task (product or product family), often on the basis of flexible re-usable units.

Assembly methods with joining elements such as screws or rivets should generally be avoided as they only increase the number of components and thereby the number of assembly operations.

★ Composing with the traditional composing elements such as screws and rivets will be used less and less. Composing methods without composing elements will enjoy increasing application; examples of this being snap locks, spot welding, ultrasonic welding, pressing, "inlaying" assembly, etc.

By far the most effective possibilities for rationalisation do not lie in selecting form of production or automation equipment, but should be sought in the product's design phase. The product's construction, component's design, choice of material and method of composing are all determined here.

★ Design for ease of assembly will attract increasing attention. Determination of product, assembly method and equipment will occur in an integrated process with the help of teamwork and project organisation.

★ Many of today's assembly tasks which are difficult to automate will be eliminated by means of the choice of other production processes.

There is a tendency towards increased diversification (spread within the product programme) and more variants. This will in turn reduce the batch size, which consequently limits the possibilities for rationalisation.

★ The building box principle used in the construction of modules for both products and assembly equipment as well as standardisation of components and sub-assemblies will be applied hand in hand with the group-technology principles.

(End of quote).

Some additional comments

The need for and interest in design for ease of assembly is noticeable today. The existence of this book is a consequence of that.

The efforts made within assembly technology to automate steadily decreasing number of pieces has lead to an interest in flexible automatic systems. The concept of "flexibility" can be understood in various ways:

★ Flexibility of the structure of equipment, i.e. equipment produced of standard equipment or as a building box system so that new machines can be built after having carried out their task.

★ Flexibility of the equipment's tools, i.e. equipment that has a particular assembly task which can be found in various products. The flexibility of the tools allows this to be accomplished. Flexibility can be achieved by versatility or adjustability.

★ Flexibility from the point of view of programming, i.e. equipment that on the basis of standard tools can be programmed for particular tasks. Industrial robots are an example of this.

★ Flexibility in adaptability, i.e. that the system can adjust and suit itself to changing conditions of assembly, e.g. that it can "see" the position of the parts itself, or select the correct components, etc.

★ Flexibility from the point of view of development, i.e. equipment that can gradually be extended from manual via mechanical to automatic assembly and which allows a suitable mixture or combination of these. Flexibility is thus available for product variations, changes in the number of pieces and in technology.

The future will be dominated by equipment possessing these characteristics mentioned. A knowledge of this and an integrated consideration of these during the design phase form an additional feature of the designer's task.

10.2 Conclusion

This publication has the task of easing the way to the assembly technique of the future. One could maintain that emphasis has been laid upon semi and fully automatic assembly, and that the book therefore promotes the view that assembly in the future will be automatic.

Whilst this is so, we must also apply whole spectrum of equipment from completely manned to fully automatic, in harmony with the technical and financial conditions which prevail.

It is maintained on several occasions that use of the design principles for mechanised assembly also leads to easier manual assembly. The book's examples and directions can therefore be used profitably in those situations where mechanisation and automation cannot be used.

We have concentrated on supplying many examples and on emphasising the basic principles of design for ease of assembly. The procedure in executing a development project in the field of assembly rationalisation has only been cited with the realisation that one does not learn about designing for ease of assembly by reading about it. It must be practised.

Word List

BASE COMPONENT

By this is understood the first component to appear in the assembly process and onto/into which, the additional components are assembled.

STORING

Time-oriented storage of unoriented components.

MOVING

Constant or step-by-step repositioning in the assembly system.

If an operator or robot carries out the moving the process will be composed of the following operations: RECOGNISE, PICK, MOVE.

FREE SURFACES

Free surfaces are those surfaces whose only function is to limit (define) the material, i.e. surfaces whose form can be changed without changing the function of the subject.

FUNCTIONAL SURFACES

Surfaces which are determined by the function of the part. If the parts function is solely the transmission of forces, then the cross sections are the functional surfaces.

HANDLING

The process or processes with the aim of moving or preparing components for composing or checking and to deliver the component to the subsequent production, assembly or packing system.

INSERTION/EXTRACTION

Positioning of component in the tool, removal of component.

COMPONENT

A component is a machine part (i.e. uncompounded) or an assembly of machine parts which are included as an object in the assembly process.

A sub-assembly can be created by a joining of machine parts and will appear as a component in the succeeding assembly operations.

CHECKING

The process or processes which check the components presence or position as well as checking the quality of the finished product. The previous processes can be accommodated in addition to particular checking operations (measuring, comparison, rejection, etc.). If the check is followed by handling or new composing operations then we can speak of ADJUSTING.

MAGAZINING

Time-oriented storage of oriented components.

MACHINE PART

A machine part is an elementary part in a machine system, produced without joining.

ASSEMBLY SURFACES

Those surfaces which serve to ensure the subjects correct connection to the rest of the system.

ALIGNMENT

Positioning of component in one or more axial directions in relation to the base component.

ORIENTATION

The process with the aim of orienting a component stream in relation to the system.

POSITIONING

Orientation of one component in relation to another.

JOINING

The process or processes with the aim of creating a (relatively) permanent connection between the components. The joining process can work by means of form, force or material. The sub-process can be handling processes in addition to special joining processes (welding, closing, cooling, etc.).

MERGING

Association of various component streams.

TRANSPORTING

The process with the aim of moving or possibly orienting components as required by the joining and checking processes.

SEPARATION

The division of stream of components into sidestreams.

TURN/ROTATE

Orientation of component in relation to the system.

Reference and Literature

(1)   LUND, T.: Konstruktion for automatisk montage.
        Rapport KL.78.68-B, AMT, DTH 1978.

(2)   HUBKA, V.: Theorie der Konstruktionsprozesse.
        Springer Verlag, Berlin 1976.

(3)   RICHTER, E., m.fl.: Montage.
        Verlag Technik, Berlin 1974.
        The book contains 375 pages and deals very thoroughly with
        the topic of assembly.

(4)   TJALVE, E.: A short course in industrial design.
        Newnes-Butterworth, London 1979.
        An inspiring, readable book on the various phases of a design
        project.

(5)   BOSCH-FMS: Das Flexible Montage-System.
        Ausgabe 2.

(6)   WARNECKE, H. J., m.fl.: Montagetechnik.
        Krausskopf-Verlag GmbH, Mainz 1975.
        Contains 137 pages on automation equipment in addition to
        102 plates of working units.

(7)   MIESE, M.: Systematische Montageplanung in Unternehmen
        mit Einzel- und Kleinserienproduktion.
        Technische Hochschule, Aachen 1973.

(8)   LöHR, H.-G.: Eine Planungsmethode für automatische
        Montagesysteme.
        Forschung und Praxis. Schriftenreihe
        Krausskopf-Verlag, Mainz 1977.
        100 pages dealing with the planning and execution of
        automatic assembly. A sound introduction providing a good
        perspective.

(9)   TIPPING, W. V.: Mechanical Assembly.
        Business Books Ltd., London 1969.

(10)   Shouryoku to Jidouka (Dec. 1972).
        Japanese magazine on rationalisation.
        A special issue was published in December 1972 on design for
        ease of assembly, totalling about 200 examples.

(11)   IVF 73817: Monteringsanpassad Konstruktion av produkter
        och detaljer.
        Sveriges Mekanförbund.

(12)   ANDREASEN, M. M., H. STAHL, E. TJALVE: Metodisk
        konstruktion.

(13)   PAHL, G. og W. BEITZ: Konstruktionslehre.
        Springer-Verlag, Berlin 1977.

(14) LUND, T.: Montageteknik.
Jernets Fremtidsprojekt – Rapport F, 1978.

(15) HESSE S./ZAPF, H.: Automatisches Fügen.
Vertrag Technik, Berlin 1972 (75 sider).
Thorough treatment of the area of automatic joining
(assembly, handling and design) as well as design of assembly
equipment.

**Literature not referred to in the book but which we also
recommend:**

ANDRESEN, U.: Ein Beitrag zum methodischen
Konstruieren bei der montagegerichten Gestaltung von
Teilen der Grosserienfertigung.
Dissertation TU, Braunschweig 1975.
Provides a survey of design for ease of assembly. Contains
principles and examples (135 pages, 77 references).

Automated Assembly.
The Institution of Production Engineers.
London W1, 1963.
A series of catalogues with sketches and proposals for
assembly equipment.

BOOTHROYD, G. and REDFORD, A. H.: Mechanised
Assembly.
McGraw-Hill Publishing Company Ltd. 1968.

DILLING, H.J., RAUSCHENBACH, T.: Rationalisierung und
Automatisierung der montage.
VDI-Verlag GmbH, Düsseldorf, 1975.
A two-volume work: Volume 1 is 260 pages long and contains
an excellent survey of the assembly field with references to
Volume 2,
a bibliography covering the years 1960-1977 (652 references).

VDI-Richtlinie 3240 Blatt 1: Zubringeeinrichtungen.
Begriffe, Kennzeichnung, Anforderungen. Oktober 1971.
121 examples of principles for realisation of assembly
operations (handling).

WARNECKE, H. J./WEISS, K.: Katalog: Zubringe-
Einrichtungen.
Krausskopf-Verlag, Mainz 1978.
Introducing section and catalogue pages (135 pages) on
handling units. Survey of German suppliers.

Werkstückhandhabung in der automatisieren Fertigung.
Würtembergischer Ingenieurverein, Stuttgart 1968.
Collection of examples (92 pages) concerning the handling of
components.